Scotland 1802-2002

figures, ideas, formations

edited by Ronald Turnbull

Edinburgh Review

Issue 110

Edinburgh Review

22a Buccleuch Place, Edinburgh, EH8 9LN
tel: 0131 651 1415
Edinburgh.Review@ed.ac.uk

MANAGING EDITOR — Ronald Turnbull
PRODUCTION MANAGER — Alexandra Wong
ADVISORY BOARD — Barbara Bryan, Stephen Carruthers, Peter Cudmore,
Karina Dent, Sam Ladkin, David Moses, Vikki Reilly
EDITORIAL BOARD — Cairns Craig, Kimberly Hutchings, A.L. Kennedy,
Andrew O'Hagan, Christopher Whyte
COVER DESIGN — Siân Braes

ISSN 0267 6672
ISBN 1 85933 207 2

PRINTED AND BOUND in the UK by Antony Rowe Ltd.,
Bumper's Farm, Chippenham, Wiltshire
PUBLISHED by the Centre for the History of Ideas in Scotland,

THE SCOTTISH ARTS COUNCIL

Introduction

Published as part of issue 110 of *Edinburgh Review*, this volume of essays on aspects of Scottish history and culture over the last two hundred years commemorates the founding of the journal bearing this name by Francis Jeffrey in 1802. The contributors include some of the most distinguished present-day commentators on Scotland, as well as a number of younger voices.

The quality of the writing in our selection of reviews from the journal in the early nineteenth century helps to explain its then phenomenal success, to which Ross Alloway alludes in his introduction. The prose is still brilliantly witty and caustic, and some of the barbs remain apposite, as when Macaulay observes that there is 'no spectacle so ridiculous as the British public in one of its periodic fits of morality'.

Certain of the essays that follow focus on important figures in modern Scottish cultural history. Robert Fraser discusses the ironic tone in the writing of J. G. Frazer, that now neglected thinker who established anthropology, and draws parallels with the stylistic complexities of David Hume. He also argues that Frazer, who as a student would have read Hume, takes from him such notions as the social usefulness of beliefs that lack rational justification. William Malcolm provides a retrospective of the life, work and politics of one of the most significant twentieth-century Scottish novelists, Lewis Grassic Gibbon. Gavin Miller supplies a necessary new statement of what is essential in the contribution of R.D.Laing to the theory and practice of psychiatry. (Incidentally, this essay also marks the 75th anniversary of Laing's birth.) An essay on Tom Nairn charts continuities and changes in the politics and theory of a thinker who over the last few decades has been central to debate about modern Scottish cultural and historical development.

Other articles deal with more general (and more popular-) cultural features and processes. Christopher Harvie ranges over a number of themes, deconstructing our various un- or semi-official national anthems, positing a sense of national victimhood, and raising doubts about the possibility of survival of cultural specificity in the face of the dominant consumerist hyperindividualism. Trevor Royle offers a reprise of the theme of Scottish militarism, or what he calls 'the love affair between the Scots and their soldiers'. Ellen-Raissa Jackson discusses dramatic and filmic representations of Scottishness, and prompts questions about what statuses and roles the Scottish film industry and theatres should have in the newly devolved Scotland.

Also on a contemporary note, in a discussion of Ashton and Ferguson's *Cover-Up of Convenience* Anthony Carty examines the difficulties involved in conducting trials such as that about Lockerbie, and probes some of the mysteries surrounding this particular case. Carty questions, no doubt controversially, whether 'international law' can in current political conditions function effectively. In his contribution to current political debate, Donald Ross, drawing on his experience as one of the unemployed, provides a report on some of the realities of the workings of the present government's so-called New Deal (or 'raw deal', as it is called by some of its supposed beneficiaries). Ross sheds light on that Kafkan world, largely ignored by the mainstream media, where the state deals with 'the socially excluded' (to use an item of the modish political gobbledegook).

This is a commemorative volume, but, as these introductory remarks indicate, one whose spirit is more critical than celebratory. Of this aspect of the collection at least, we hope, Francis Jeffrey would have approved.

Selections from
The Edinburgh Review

introduced by
Ross Alloway

The first review bearing the name *The Edinburgh Review* was published in 1755 with a design to 'lay before the Public, from time to time, a view of the progressive state of learning in this country'. To that end, a young Adam Smith reviewed Samuel Johnson's *A Dictionary of the English Language*:

> The present undertaking is very extensive. A dictionary of the English language, however useful, or rather necessary, has never been hitherto attempted with the least degree of success. To explain hard words and terms of art seems to have been the chief purpose of all the former compositions which have borne the title of English dictionaries. Mr. Johnson has extended his views very much farther, and has made a very full collection of all the different meanings of each English word, justified by examples from authors of good reputation. When we compare this book with other dictionaries, the merit of its author appears very extraordinary.

Reviewing in the first *Edinburgh* was conceived as more than a mere objective recommendation or condemnation of books for public consumption, but also as a public space for demonstrating the reviewer's erudition and intelligence. Thus after his positive preamble, Smith proceeds to 'take notice of some defects' by first listing them and then detailing for numerous pages how he would have written the dictionary. Unfortunately for the sake of the first *Edinburgh*, Smith's demonstration was characteristic of other reviews to be found in its pages: at best dry and at worst hair-splitting. It failed after only two numbers. It seemed that if one were to lay a view 'before the public', the prose had better be compelling.

When the title *The Edinburgh Review* was resurrected in October 1802, its contributors certainly used its pages as a forum for demonstrating their intelligence, but could by no means be accused of tedium. Its first editor, Francis Jeffrey, was a master of incisive prose. Primarily remembered now for being 'wrong' about Wordsworth, he was at least certain of his position. Indeed it is easy to criticise from a distance; a luxury the reviewers did not have. Books were being published and the *Edinburgh* offered its views to the public. It is convenient now—especially when many of the reviews are not widely available—to see a dislike of Wordsworth as a critical blunder, but it should not be forgotten that Wordsworth's poems were not all as accomplished as 'Tintern Abbey'. One particularly poor performance, 'Alice Fell', certainly merited Jeffrey's spite: 'If the printing of such trash as this be not felt as an insult on the public taste, we are afraid it cannot be insulted.' While from a twentieth-century perspective certain reviews may seem obtuse, the striking prose of many reviews demands a reassessment. Indeed the most capable justification of positions espoused in the *Edinburgh* are in the reviews themselves. At the height of the *Edinburgh*'s popularity nineteenth-century readers so valued its judgments that a print run of 14,000 could hardly fill the demand for its criticism, so that when bound into volumes and sold as books, some volumes went through ten editions. Of course, given that many of its writers were among the most important critics, essayists, historians and artists of the nineteenth century, its popularity should hardly surprise us now. In its pages, soon-to-be-famous writers were given an opportunity to exercise their pen via vivid biographies, deflating unqualified pomposity or by protecting the national intestine from curiously patriotic cooks. Reprinted below are several neglected reviews from only a few of *The Edinburgh Review*'s distinguished collaborators: Macaulay on Byron, Hazlitt on Coleridge and Sir Walter Scott on cookbooks.

Thomas Babington Macaulay, June 1831. From a review of *Letters and Journals of Lord Byron: with Notices of his Life.*

In the rank of Lord Byron, in his understanding, in his character, in his very person, there was a strange union of opposite extremes. He was born to all that men covet and admire. But in every one of those eminent advantages which he possessed over others, there was mingled something of misery and debasement. He was sprung from a house, ancient indeed and noble, but degraded and impoverished by a series of crimes and follies, which had attained a scandalous publicity. The kinsman whom he succeeded had died poor, and, but for merciful judges, would have died upon the gallows. The young peer had great intellectual powers; yet there was an unsound part in his mind. He had naturally a generous and tender heart; but his temper was wayward and irritable. He had a head which statuaries loved to copy, and a foot, the deformity of which beggars in the streets mimicked. Distinguished at once by the strength and by the weakness of his intellect, affectionate yet perverse, a poor lord, and a handsome cripple, he required, if ever a man required, the firmest and the most judicious training. But capriciously as nature had dealt with him, the relative to whom the office of forming his character was intrusted, was more capricious still. At one time she stifled him with her caresses—at another time she insulted his deformity. He came into the world, and the world treated him as his mother treated him— sometimes with kindness, sometimes with severity, never with justice. It indulged him without discrimination, and punished him without discrimination. He was truly a spoiled child,—not merely the spoiled child of his parent, but the spoiled child of nature, the spoiled child of fortune, the spoiled child of fame, the spoiled child of society. His first poems were received with a contempt which, feeble as they were, they did not actually deserve. The poem which he published in this return from his travels, was, on the other hand, extolled far above its merit. At twenty-four, he found himself on the highest pinnacle of literary fame, with Scott, Wordsworth, Southey, and a crowd of other distinguished writers, beneath his feet. There is scarcely an instance in history of so sudden a rise to so dizzy an eminence.

Everything that could stimulate, and everything that could gratify the strongest propensities of our nature—the gaze of a hundred drawingrooms, the acclamations of the whole nation, the applause of applauded men, the love of the loveliest women—all of this world, and all the glory of it, were at once offered to a young man to whom nature had given violent passions, and whom education had never taught to control them. He lived as many men live who have no similar excuses to plead for their faults. But his countrymen and his countrywomen would love him and admire him. They were resolved to see in his excesses only the flash and outbreak of that same fiery mind which glowed in his poetry. He attacked religion; yet in religious circles his name was mentioned with fondness, and in many religious publications his works were censured with singular tenderness. He lampooned the prince regent; yet he could not alienate the Tories. Everything, it seemed, was to be forgiven youth, rank, and genius.

Then came the reaction. Society, capricious in its indignations as it had been capricious in its fondness, flew in a rage with its forward and petted darling. He had been worshipped with an irrational idolatry. He was persecuted with an irrational fury. Much has been written about those unhappy domestic occurrences which decided the fate of his life. Yet nothing is, nothing ever was positively known to the public, but this,—that he quarreled with his lady, and that she refused to live with him… We know of no spectacle so ridiculous as the British public in one of its periodic fits of morality. In general, elopements, divorces, and family quarrels, pass with little notice. We read the scandal, talk about it for a day, and forget it. But once in six or seven years, our virtue becomes outrageous. We cannot suffer the laws of religion and decency to be violated. We must make a stand against vice. We must teach libertines, that the English people appreciate the importance of domestic ties. Accordingly, some unfortunate man, in no respect more depraved than hundreds whose offences have been treated with lenity, is singled out as an expiatory sacrifice. If he has children, they are to be taken from him. If he has a profession, he is to be driven from it. He is cut by the higher orders, and hissed by the lower. He is in truth, a sort of whipping-boy, by whose vicarious agonies, all the other transgressors of the same class are, it is supposed, sufficiently, chastised. We reflect very complacently on our own severity, and compare with great pride the high standard of morals established in England, with the Parisian laxity. At length, our anger is satiated. Our victim is ruined and heart-broken. And our virtue goes quietly to sleep for seven years more… The obloquy which Byron had to endure, was such as might well have shaken a more constant mind. The newspapers were filled with lampoons. The theatres shook with execrations. He was excluded from circles where he had lately been the observed of all observers. All those creeping things that riot in the decay of nobler natures, hastened to their repast; and they were right;—they did after their kind. It is not every day that the savage envy of aspiring dunces is gratified by the agonies of such a spirit, and the degradation of such a name.

The unhappy man left his country for ever. The howl of contumely followed him across the sea, up the Rhine, over the Alps; it gradually waxed fainter; it died away. Those who had raised it began to ask each other, what, after all, was the matter about which they had been so clamorous; and wished to invite back the criminal whom they had just chased from them. His poetry became more popular than it had ever been; and his complaints were read with tears by thousands and tens of thousands who had never seen his face.

He had fixed his home on the shores of the Adriatic, in the most picturesque and interesting of cities, beneath the brightest of skies, and by the brightest of seas. Censoriousness was not the vice of the neighbors he had chosen… From the public opinion of the country of his adoption, he had nothing to dread. With the public opinion of the country of his birth, he was at open war. He plunged into wild and desperate excesses, ennobled by no generous or tender sentiment. From his Venetian haram he sent forth volume after volume, full of eloquence, of wit, of pathos, of ribaldry, and of bitter disdain. His health sank under the effects of his intemperance. His hair turned grey. His food ceased to nourish him. A hectic fever withered him up. It seemed that his body and mind were about to perish together…

Sick of inaction,—degraded in his own eyes by his private vices, and by his literary failures,—pining for untried excitement and honourable distinction,—he carried his exhausted body and his wounded spirit to the Grecian camp. His conduct in his new situation showed so much vigour and good sense as to justify us believing, that, if his life had been prolonged, he might have distinguished himself as a soldier and a politician. But pleasure and sorrow had done the work of seventy years upon his delicate frame. The hand of death was on him: he knew it; and the only wish which he uttered was that he might die sword in hand. This was denied to him. Anxiety, exertion, exposure, and those fatal stimulants which had become indispensable to him, soon stretched him on a sickbed, in a strange land, amidst strange faces, without one human being that he loved near him. There, at thirty-six, the most celebrated Englishman of the nineteenth century closed his brilliant and miserable career…

It is always difficult to separate the literary character of a man who lives in our own time from his personal character. It is peculiarly difficult to make this separation in the case of Lord Byron. For it is scarcely too much to say, that Lord Byron never wrote without some reference, direct or indirect, to himself. The interest excited by the events of his life, mingles itself in our minds, and probably in the minds of almost all our readers, with the interest which properly belongs to his works. A generation must pass away before it will be possible to form a fair judgment of his books, considered merely as books. At present they are not only books, but relics…

Among that large class of young persons whose reading is almost entirely confined to works of the imagination, the popularity of Lord Byron was unbounded. They bought pictures of him; they treasured up the smallest relics of him; they learned his poems by heart, and did their best to write like him, and to look like him. Many of them practised at the glass, in the hope of catching the curl of the upper lip, and the scowl of the brow, which appear in some of his portraits. A few discarded their neckcloths, in imitation of their great leader. For some years the Minerva press sent forth no novel without a mysterious, unhappy, Lara-like peer. The number of hopeful undergraduates and medical students who became things of dark imaginings,—on whom the freshness of the heart ceased to fall like dew,—whose passions had consumed themselves to dust, and to whom the relief of tears was denied, passes all calculation. This was not the worst. There was created in the minds of many of these enthusiasts, a pernicious and absurd association between intellectual power and moral depravity. From the poetry of Lord Byron they drew a system of ethics, compounded of misanthropy and voluptuousness; a system in which the two great commandments were, to hate your neighbour, and to love your neighbour's wife.

This affectation has passed away; and a few more years will destroy whatever yet remains of that magical potency which once belonged to the name of Byron. To us he is still a man, young, noble, and unhappy. To our children he will merely be a writer; and their impartial judgment will appoint his place among writers, without regard to his rank, or to his private history. That his poetry will undergo a severe sifting; that much of what has been admired by his contemporaries will be rejected as worthless, we have little doubt. But we have as little doubt, that, after the closest scrutiny, there will still remain much that can only perish with the English language.

William Hazlitt, September 1816. From a review of *Christabel: Kubla Khan,* *a Vision. The Pains of Sleep* **by Samuel Taylor Coleridge.**

The advertisement by which this work was announced to the publick, carried in its front a recommendation from Lord Byron,—who it seems, has somewhere praised Christabel, as 'a wild and singularly original and beautiful poem'. Great as the noble bard's merits undoubtedly are in poetry, some of his latest publications dispose us to distrust his authority, where the question is what ought to meet the public eye; and the works before us afford an additional proof, that his judgement on such matters is not absolutely to be relied on. Moreover, we are a little inclined to doubt the value of the praise which one poet lends another. It seems now-a-days to be the practice of that once irritable race to laud each other without bounds; and one can hardly avoid suspecting, that what is thus lavishly advanced may be laid out with a view to being repaid with interest. Mr. Coleridge, however, must be judged by his own merits...

Kubla Khan is given to the public, it seems, 'at the request of a poet of great and deserved celebrity;'—but whether Lord Byron the praiser of 'the Christabel,' or the Laureate, the praiser of Princes, we are not informed. As far as Mr Coleridge's 'own opinions are concerned,' it is published, 'not upon the ground of any poetic merits,' but 'as a PSYCHOLOGICAL CURIOSITY!' In these opinions of the candid author, we entirely concur; but for this reason we hardly think it was necessary to give the minute detail which the Preface contains, of the circumstances attending its composition. Had the question regarded 'Paradise Lost,' or 'Dryden's Ode,' we could not have had a more particular account of the circumstances in which it was composed. It was in the year 1797, and in the summer season. Mr Coleridge was in bad health;— the particular disease is not given; but the careful reader will form his own conjectures. He had retired very prudently to a lonely farm-house; and whoever would see the place which gave birth to the 'psychological curiosity,' may find his way thither without a guide; for it is situated on the confines of Somerset and Devonshire, and on the Exmoor part of the boundary; and it is, moreover, between Porlock and Linton. In that farm-house, he had a slight indisposition, and had taken an anodyne, which threw him into a deep sleep in his chair, (whether after dinner or not he omits to state), 'at the moment that he was reading a sentence in Purchas's Pilgrims,' relative to a palace of Kubla Khan. The effects of the anodyne, and the sentence together, were prodigious: They produced the 'curiosity' now before us; for, during his three-hours sleep, Mr Coleridge 'has the most vivid confidence that he could not have composed less than from two to three hundred lines.' On awaking, he 'instantly and eagerly' wrote down the verses here published; when he was (he says, 'unfortunately') called out by a 'person on business from Porlock, and detained by above an hour;' and when he returned, the vision was gone. The lines here given smell strongly, it must be owned, of the anodyne; and, but that an under dose of a sedative produces contrary effects, we should inevitably have been lulled by them into forgetfulness of all things. Perhaps a dozen more such lines as the following would reduce the most irritable of critics to a state of inaction.

'A damsel with a dulcimer
In a vision once I saw:
It was an Abyssinian maid
And on her dulcimer she play'd,
Singing of Mount Abora.
Could I revive within me
Her symphony and song,
To such a deep delight 'twould win
That with music loud and long,
I would build that dome in air,
That sunny dome! those caves of ice!
And all who heard should see them there,
And all should cry, Beware! Beware!
His flashing eyes, his floating hair!
Weave a circle round him thrice,
And close your eyes with holy dread:
For he on honey-dew hath fed,' &c. &c.

There is a good deal more altogether as exquisite—and in particular a fine description of a wood, 'ancient as the hills;' and 'folding sunny spots of greenery!' But we suppose this specimen will be sufficient.

Persons in this poet's unhappy condition, generally feel the want of sleep as the worst of their evils; but there are instances, too, in the history of the disease, of sleep being attended with new agony, as if the waking thoughts, how wild and turbulent soever, had still been under some slight restraint,

13

which sleep instantly removed. Mr Coleridge appears to have experienced this symptom, if we may judge from the title of his third poem, 'The Pains of Sleep;' and, in truth, from its composition—which is mere raving, without any thing more affecting than a number of incoherent words, expressive of extravagance and incongruity.—We need give no specimen of it.

Upon the whole, we look upon this publication as one of the most notable pieces of impertinence of which the press has lately been guilty; and one of the boldest experiments that has yet been made on the patience or understanding of the public. It is impossible, however, to dismiss it, without a remark or two. The other productions of the Lake School have generally exhibited talents thrown away upon subjects so mean, that no power of genius could ennoble them; or perverted and rendered useless by a false theory of poetical composition. But even in the worst of them, if we except the 'White Doe' of Mr Wordsworth and some of the laureate odes, there were always some gleams of feeling or of fancy. But the thing now before us, is utterly destitute of value. It exhibits from beginning to end not a ray of genius; and we defy any man to point out a passage of poetical merit in any of the three pieces which it contains, except, perhaps, the following lines in p.32, and even these are not very brilliant; nor is the leading thought original—

'Alas! They had been friends in youth;
But whispering tongues can poison truth;
And constancy lives in realms above;
And life is thorny; and youth is vain;
And to be wroth with one we love,
Doth work like madness in the brain.'

With this one exception, there is literally not one couplet in the publication before us which would be reckoned poetry, or even sense, were it found in the corner of a newspaper or upon the window of an inn. Must we then be doomed to hear such a mixture of raving and driv'ling, extolled as the work of a 'wild and original' genius, simply because Mr Coleridge has now and then written fine verses, and a brother poet chooses, in his milder mood, to laud him from courtesy or from interest?

Sir Walter Scott, July 1805. From a review of *The New Practice of Cookery, Pastry, Baking and Preserving, Being the Country Housewife's Best Friend* and *Receipts in Modern Cookery.*

It seems to have been a complaint familiar in the mouths of our ancestors, and which we have too often seen cause to re-echo in the present day, 'That God sends good meat, but the devil sends cooks.' The irritability, the obstinacy, and the perfidy of the present culinary race, indeed, obviously demonstrate their ascent from regions even hotter than those which they occupy upon earth; and, while the direct attacks of the arch-enemy are opposed and counteracted by the clergy, who may be considered as the regular forces to whom our defence is entrusted, it is with pleasure we see a disposition, in the learned and experienced among the laity, to volunteer against the hordes of greasy Cossacks whom he detaches to those quarters, as marauders upon our daily patience and our annual income.

In first entering the field upon this occasion, we had some difficulty to settle the rank of these auxiliaries amongst themselves, or, to drop the metaphor, we were at a loss, after considering the high claims to attention preferred by both publications, to which we ought to give the precedence in our critique. It is true, Mesdames Hudson and Donat prefer a bold claim to the grateful recollection of those who have regaled on their dainties. 'It becomes them not,' as they are modestly pleased to express it, 'to judge of their own merit; but with honest confidence they appeal to a numerous list of subscribers, who have eat and judged of their works.' In this passage there is some ambiguity. If, by this intimation, it is meant that the subscribers actually eat the volume to which they subscribed, we, the Reviewers, will frankly tell Mrs Hudson and Mrs Donat, that, notwithstanding the evangelical authority which may be quoted for this literary diet, we cannot bring our stomachs to submit to it, especially as in one sense, we are already obliged to devour many more works than we are well able to digest. On the other hand, if the judgement referred to was formed from actually partaking of the dishes analysed in this volume, we only want the opportunity, happily enjoyed by these subscribers, conscientiously to join in their verdict. Upon the slightest intimation, the long coach shall convey our critical fraternity to the hospitable mansion where these fair dames have presided, and do preside, over the good things of the earth; and the—*fiat experimentum*!...

The prefatory advertisement to this book is too interesting to be suppressed. It shows at once the deep learning of the ladies by whom it was written; their honest sense of the dignity of their vocation; and their laudable zeal for its being conducted on the true principles of the British constitution, as well as upon those of sound experimental philosophy.

The late Dr Black, Professor of Chemistry in the University of Edinburgh, has instructed and enlightened the world by his philosophical, ingenious, and patient researches in that science, which somewhere in his works he has defined to be 'the effect of heat and mixture upon bodies.'

This definition applies as directly to the cook as to the chemist: His kitchen is his school, his boilers, his digesters; his stoves, and not forgetting his cradle-spit, correspond to the crucible, the alembic, the retort, and other apparatus of the chemist; and both are equally applied to prove the effect of heat and mixture upon bodies. It must be admitted, at the same time, that the range or kingdom of the bodies they severally operate upon, are wonderfully different. The chemist gropes below ground, and in the dark, through the mineral kingdom: while the cook operates in the light, and above board, upon the animal and the vegetable world.

The judges also who are to decide upon the result of their several experiments, are not less different and opposite, than the subjects they have operated upon. The chemist lays his experiments, stuffed generally with mathematical demonstrations, or the more abstruse calculations of the minus and plus of algebra, before some Royal Society, composed of a few meagre philosophers, 'with spectacles on nose;' while the judges the cook appeals to are all the jolly *bons vivants* in the Imperial Kingdom; and his compounds are drawn from every thing that is delicate and high flavoured in the animal and in the vegetable world; and, without any other demonstration than what his larding and his sauces give, he appeals directly to the sound and nice palate of his numerous judges...

They have subjoined many valuable receipts in housekeeping, for curing beef, for making of hams and bacon, for the dairy, and pastry-baking, and the best receipt for artificial yeast, which can be made and used the same day, and does not make the bread sour; all of which they have practised at Smeaton with wonderful success. In short, they now offer to the world, not a cobweb theory of cookery; such as the flimsy constitution-mongers of France have spun for these twelve or fifteen years past out of their distempered brains, to deceive and ruin that miserable people: No! here, facts only are narrated and by correct attention to the directions given, the cook, whether male or female, may rest assured of meeting the approbation of the nicest and most delicate palate; and will prove particularly useful for those who reside in the country. The different receipts for making the India currie powder and pellow, are taken from the best practice of their native country.

From this advertisement, much extraordinary information may be derived. We have already noticed, that there is great room to believe that the subscribers, to testify their approbation of the contents, actually ate the book; like the man who, in his zealous applause of roast beef, devoured the spit from which it had been taken. But this is not all. We are informed, in point of historical fact, that the various legislators of France have, for these twelve or fifteen years past, been busily engaged in digesting systems of cookery. And, truly, though this is mentioned in rather derogating terms, on account, apparently, of their bad success, we consider the fact to be, on the whole, a discovery in their favour, since, for our own parts, we never suspected them to be so usefully or innocently employed. It is a fact of subordinate importance, but nevertheless somewhat curious, that the whole Royal Society make use of one pair of spectacles, placed on the nose, doubtless, of the President. We have long observed an unvaried coincidence in the views and pursuits of this learned body, and are happy to be able to trace it to a cause equally unsuspected and satisfactory.

As to the receipts which follow this curious and instructive preface, they are distinctly expressed; and from the well known hospitality and elegance of the family in which they were composed, we have no doubt they will be found admirable. We must observe, however, that they are arranged in rather a miscellaneous order; for after a receipt to make 'a half-peck bun,' we pass abruptly to another which begins, 'The slacked lime must be well sifted and steeped in a pit, ' &c. &c.; and again, 'Take two shovels full of coarse water sand, one ditto of hammer slag well sifted, one ditto powdered brick dust, &c. Now, although we are specially directed that the former mixture shall be wrought into 'thin porridge,' and the latter made neither 'too fat nor too poor,' yet, we are somewhat inclined to doubt, whether any management or attention in the preparation, could render them digestible by human stomachs, or, indeed, whether they can be strictly said to belong to the arts of cookery, pasty-baking, or preserving, unless the ladies are of opinion with the Copper Captain, that 'a piece of buttered wall is excellent.' Other receipts occur, in

17

which 'an ounce of white arsenic,' and the 'expressed juice of the deadly nightshade,' are the chief ingredients. These, we were at first glance inclined to suppose borrowed from the French systems already mentioned,—perhaps the original recipe for a restorative cordial à *l'hopital*, or a *fricandeau à Touissaint*,—if indeed, the patriotic composers did not design them for the regale of the Emperor himself on his long announced visit.

The very errata of this work evince the care and deep science of the compilers. Some corrections refer to the ingredients; and it will be prudent to attend to them specially, as the error, according to the phrase of the Civilians, is sometimes *in substantialibus*. Thus, we have 'for linen read lemon;' 'for chicken, read onion;' 'for pepper, read paper.' Others regard accessories; as 'after raspberries (in a receipt for making jam) add, together with two pounds and a half raw sugar:' or, 'for mix it all with the foregoing ingredients, read and mix them with a mutchkin and a half of brandy.' Others refer to proportion: as, 'for pint and a half, read bit;' and, 'for half a, read three thirds.' This last correction appeared to us to conceal some new and abstract doctrine in fractions, adopted perhaps from the facetious Costard; for ladies acquainted with philosophy cannot be ignorant of Shakespeare.—'Biron. Three times three is nine. Costard. Not so, Sir; under correction, I hope it is not so. Biron. By Jove, I always took three threes for nine. Costard. O Lord, Sir, it were a pity you should get your living by reckoning, Sir.'

Ballads—or Blues— of the Nation?

Christopher Harvie

I THE NATIONAL CAUSE REVIVED

Early 2002, three years into devolution, and the land lies uneasy. Reshufflings of the Scottish Executive, dwindling interest in politics particularly among the young, threats to Scottish representation at Westminster and the formulae for Scottish expenditure, portend an ill-tempered confrontation. Polls show increasingly divergent views about nationality. 'British Scottishness' seems on the way out.

There are hints of a reviving ethnic nationalism. Tom Devine's *The Scottish Nation*, well-received in 1999, endorsed the Campaign for a Scottish Assembly's *Claim of Right for Scotland* (1986) after hurrying past the 'great age' of unionist industrialisation. Tom Nairn in *After Britain: New Labour and the Return of Scotland* (1999) revised an earlier view that arguing with a nationalist was like 'being pinned to a bar by a drunk'. Now (the drunk having sobered up a bit) some of his old tropes were being given a more admiring reprise:

> As a collective identity or 'community', a nation is in fact defined by a complex skein of relationships between 'high' and 'low', and in the case of a small and ancient nation such relationships were close. Their permanent dislocation could not fail to produce an analogous disruption

of outlook and judgement, a sundered mentality which henceforth had to function on two levels.

This was the metaphorical wound out of which the underground stream had surged, as from a structural and now inescapable disablement. In the longer reach of time it is what appears as the river of loss: corrosive, numbing, and seeping relentlessly through the foundation of every Scottish generation since then.

The 'poor little Scotland' of the Declaration of Arbroath hovered around, even though the Scottish parliament was savaged by Europe's most primitive tabloids. It kept ahead of all-but-forgotten Westminster but its political culture had yet to provide a civic remedy for disjuncture of non-federal devolution, leaving this to the 'shuttlefolk' who commuted to the metropolis and who, at the other end constituted—in Blair and his Anglo-Scots milieu— the most centralising oligarchy Britain has yet seen.

Ethnic inflection gained significance in a post-industrial state where 'cultural politics', tourism and sport grew more salient, making one aspect of popular patriotism worth a second look. Nations have anthems; regions or city-states have not. Scotland has a choice at least three: 'Scots wha hae', composed by Burns in 1793 but these days less present than one might think, (footnote: it doesn't figure in www.nationalanthems.com.) 'Scotland the Brave' (still to be heard on the BBC each morning, in the British medley), a blameless piece of touristic kitsch—

> Land of the purple heather,
> Land of the foaming river,
> Land of my heart forever,
> Scotland the brave!

concocted by Cliff Hanley in the 1950s, and 'Flower of Scotland', written by Robin Williamson of the folk group the Corries in 1968, vaguely Burnsian in its sentiments, and sung along to a tune akin to the slaves' chorus in Verdi's *Aida*:

> O flower of Scotland!
> When will we see
> Your like again?

Who fought and died for
Your wee bit hill and glen,
And stood against him,
Proud Edward's army,
And sent him homeward
Tae think again.

The hills are bare now
And autumn leaves lie thick and still
O'er land that is lost now
Which those so dearly held,
And stood...

These days are passed now,
And in the past they must remain.
But we can still rise now
And be the nation again
That stood...

'Flower' has become the 'SNP song'. It retaliates for 'God save the Queen' at football and rugby matches, just as the saltire or lion rampant have crowded out the Union Jack. Yet it remains as worrying an encounter as the website of the *Daily Record*. If John O'Leary told Yeats that there were 'certain things a man must not do to save his country', the 'Flower' seems an anthology of them: derivative not just of Burns but of Milton ('thick as the autumn leaves on Vallombroso') historically inaccurate, ungrammatical, without rhyme, and pickled in sentimentality. It's only utility is the slow upward drive of its first syllable, perfectly attuned to the 'Ahhhawww' of a well-oiled football crowd.

The survival of 'God save the Queen' until the 1970s was always odd. Composed around 1740, perhaps by Henry Carey, it took off during the Jacobite crisis of 1745. Mostly dynastic grovelling, when it got nationalistic it got nasty. Its fourth stanza instructs God:

Lord grant that Marshal WADE
May by thy Mighty Aid
Victory bring.
May he Sedition hush,

And like a Torrent rush,
Rebellious Scots to crush,
God save the King.

Yet its historical twin was 'Rule Britannia' (also 1740) by the Augustan Scot and part-creator of English literature, James Thomson of Ednam, the first of several transferred patriots. In 1801, only eight years after 'Scots wha hae', another Scottish radical, Thomas Campbell, wrote 'Ye mariners of England' and in the 1840s yet another, Charles MacKay, wrote 'Cheer boys, cheer!' and 'England over all!'

Chancers, traitors, or patriots *in their way*? Campbell wrote 'Ye Mariners' (he had not actually visited England) along with 'An exile of Erin' sympathising with the Irish rising of 1798, and died revered by the Poles. MacKay, editor of the *Illustrated London News*, spent his later life campaigning for Gaelic poetry. Robert Crawford argues that eighteenth-century Scots created English literature. (Crawford, 1992, 16-44) Did they also coin an 'Imperial song' which was masculine and positive compared with a Scottish patriotism—Jacobite songs composed after the cause was safely dead or Lady Nairne's post-Flodden *tristesse* in 'The Flowers of the Forest'—gone winsome. (Donaldson, 1993)

This is an uneasy proposition about national culture, not simplified when we deconstruct Burns's key contribution:

Scots, wha hae wi' WALLACE bled,
Scots, wham BRUCE has aften led;
Welcome to your gory bed,—
Or to victorie.—

Now's the day, and now's the hour;
See the front o' battle lower;
See approach proud EDWARD's power—
Chains and Slaverie!

Wha will be a traitor—knave?
Wha can fill a coward's grave!
Wha sae base as be a Slave?
—Let him turn and flee!

Wha for SCOTLAND's king & law
Freedom's sword will strongly draw,
FREE-MAN stand, or FREE-MAN fa',
Let him follow me.—

By Oppression's woes and pains!
By your Sons in servile chains!
We will drain our dearest veins,
But they shall be free!

Lay the proud Usurpers low!
Tyrants fall in every foe!
LIBERTY's in every blow!
Let us DO—or DIE!

This is less simple, and less ethnic, than it looks. Burns' opening in Stanza One is a statement of fact, rather than the rousing command 'Allons, enfants de la Patrie!' which starts the 'Marseillaise'—though it still sounds like a command, Gaelic slogan or war-cry. It remembers martyrs and liberators, anticipating sacrifice before eventual triumph. The comparatively downbeat mood continues in Stanza Two; the looming crisis isn't Rouget de L'Isle's 'le jour de gloire est arrivé' but the grimmer 'see the front o' battle lower', with the threat of enslavement contending against national pride. Stanza Three presents a choice: become a traitor, coward or slave—and in his pre-Bannockburn career Bruce had arguably been all three—by taking the chance of flight, or risk death by fighting for the right. Stanza Four goes from this to establish a sort of social compact in the style of the Declaration of Arbroath, 1320, via Archdeacon Barbour's long narrative poem *The Brus* of 1376. 'Scotland's king and law' are to be fought for: aided by the strength which comes from being a freeman and fighting for freedom. The alternative is stated in Stanza Five: oppression, pain and slavery will continue until Scotland gains freedom by blood sacrifice. Stanza Six is the only one to use an ethnic argument. Ursurpation by the English transfers guilt to individual English soldiers: 'Tyrants fall in every foe'. These lines, Burns wrote, were taken not from Barbour but from the later and much more aggressively anti-English Blind Hary's *The Wallace* (c. 1476). The final couplet states that national liberty demands success or death, but by embodying the motto of the

Douglases 'Doe or die!' sounds a less-than-reassuring echo of where over-mighty nobles would later get the country.

The song in fact posits choices, not the ascriptive attitude 'you are Scots, you must do this' as in the ethnic patriotism of 'La Marseillaise', which was composed a year earlier, in April 1792, and became widespread after the insurrection of 10 August. Burns wrote 'Scots wha hae' five months after the execution of Louis XVI on 21 January, 1793, and the declaration of war on Britain in the following month, yet it was not published in, or politically directed at, Scotland. Burns sent it, anonymously and much later, to the London *Morning Chronicle*, a Whig daily. It appeared on 8 May 1794, when the confrontation between the English Friends of the People and the government appeared imminent. Four years after Burns' death 'Scots wha hae' was printed in Currie's edition and praised by the Whig composer Robert Nares, Archdeacon of Lichfield, although he deprecated the poem's connection with French radicalism. In 1841 Thomas Moore would speak of it as 'a song which in a great national crisis, would be of more avail than all the eloquence of a Demosthenes.' Its Scottish identity was more enigmatic.

II BURNS AND PHILOCTETES

When the Scottish parliament opened on July 1 1999, 'Scots wha hae' was not sung, but the blamelessly internationalist, though not entirely non-sexist 'A Man's a Man for a' That'. The poet-patriot had, in the interim, rarely been absent from Scottish affairs, though the enlightenment intellectual was never as popular as the hedonistic romantic—'him that lay with nearly as many women as Solomon did, though not all at one time'—nailed in *Cloud Howe* by Lewis Grassic Gibbon. The former is more in evidence in 'Scots wha hae' : the youth who, with other farmers' sons, was privately tutored by John Murdoch, and read Adam Smith, both the *Treatise on Moral Sentiments* (1759) and *The Wealth of Nations* (1776). Burns marvelled at Smith, and it is Smithian ideas which underly the idea of contract and mutuality in 'Scots wha hae' and other poems, for example, the 'Epistle to J. Lapraik' (1786):

But ye whom social pleasure charms,
   Whose hearts the tide of kindness warms,
   Who hold your being on the terms,
       'Each aid the others.'

Come to the bowl, come to my arms,
My friends, my brothers!

Smith's 'sympathy' gives a 'composure' to most of Burns' poems, most notoriously in 'The Cottar's Saturday Night'. This near-parodic bit of rustic Augustan is about a class which would be dead almost before Burns himself. Elsewhere reality forced itself on him, as in 'To a Mouse', in which the little animal dehoused by the coulter of his plough is compared with the poet's own failure to establish himself on a farm:

But thou art blest compared with me
The present only troubles thee
While oh! I backward cast my 'ee
On prospects drear
But forward, tho' I canna see,
I guess and fear.

In a political context, this is untenable self-pity. The Irish critic Luke Gibbons comments that Smithian 'sympathy', a learned drive towards the conscious and rational presentation of the individual, opposed itself to the emotional self-degradation of Philoctetes, who displayed his wounds to excite sympathy. This accusation was frequently levelled at the Irish (Gibbons, 281), and certainly reflected in their own anthems 'The Wearing of the Green' (1798), whose theme of victimhood is repeated in T D Sullivan's 'God save Ireland' (1867)

'To a Mouse' is Burns in Philoctetic mode. By contrast, 'Scots wha hae', though drawing on patriotic sources, presents a politics of choice. Burns' enemy is not named as English, the breach with them remains civic, not ethnic. In this he consciously echoes the Declaration of Arbroath which, Ted Cowan has argued, reflects Bruce's own Anglo-Norman background and preoccupations common to both countries. Before 1066 the Scots had fought the Welsh, the Irish, the Northumbrians and the Norse. Thereafter the Anglo-Normans, preoccupied with their French possessions, had been on the whole favourably neutral. Proud Edward, the father of the enemy at Bannockburn, had disrupted the balance, but it could be rearranged in this Whig fashion.

The result has a lot in common with Thomson's 'Rule Britannia', Thomson being another of Burns' enthusiasms:

When Britain first, at heaven's command,
    Arose from out the azure main;
This was the charter of the land,
    And guardian angels sung this strain:
        'Rule, Britannia, rule the waves;
        Britons never will be slaves.'

This constitutional patriotism is similar to the contract element—'king and law' in Burns—and also agnostic about England, although it originally featured in a play *Alfred* in which 'Britain' could only have been a remote notion. The concepts Burns regarded as alien are all there: slavery, autocracy, ill-disposed foreigners, internal weaknesses. Thomson's Whig argument is amplified in his longer poem 'Liberty' (1736):

        …Theirs the triumph be,
By deep *Invention's* keen pervading eye,
The heart of courage, and the Hand of Toil,
Each conquer'd ocean staining with their blood,
Instead of Treasure robb'd' by ruffian War,
Round social Earth to circle fair Exchange,
And bind the Nations in a golden Chain.

Burns was certainly expansive in his Whiggery, responsive to the demands of the Scots *menu peuple*, which became acute with agricultural improvement and industrialisation. Although many of the arguments in 'Scots wha hae' parallel those of Sir David Lindsay's 'John the Commonweal' in *The Three Estates* (1544) —the plunder of the 'folk above', and the landlords barring the people's right to 'come into the body of the kirk'—the play doesn't seem to have been known to Burns. He was influenced by the Tory and Jacobite Robert Fergusson, with Allan Ramsay's *Gentle Shepherd* (1725) and Bolingbroke's *Patriot King* (c.1740), but also by the Covenanters, the sense of a common democratic struggle being brought out in another short poem:

    The Solemn League and Covenant
    Now brings a smile, now brings a tear,
    But sacred freedom then was theirs.
    If thou'rt a slave, indulge your sneer.

Burns meant not the National Covenant of 1638 but the 1643 agreement between the Scots and English parliaments, and thus endorses a 'British' identity similar to Thomson's. Even treason fits in here, as part of an Enlightenment notion. In his earlier ballad 'A Parcel of Rogues' he attacked the destruction of the Scots parliament in 1707:

> The English steel we could disdain
> Secure in valour's station.
> But English gold has been our bane
> Such a parcel of rogues in a nation.

But this also fitted into the arguments of Smith and Ferguson, that the actual fruits of commerce could themselves lead to 'luxury and corruption'.

Burns' language betrays the difficulty of establishing a populist patriotism, when the nature of the state is founded not on ethnie but on negotiation. This inhibits the emotional appeal and the allure of martyrdom. English gold, or French gold, is part of the negotiation and can't be wished away. Money—David Marquand's 'universal pander'—and career make adherence to a simple patriotism difficult. Deconstruct 'Scots wha hae' and we find, besides nationalism, Whiggery, Freemasonry, Bolingbrokism: ideas not all remote from those of the Edinburgh Reviewers of 1802.

In its religious or feudal-covenant form, Burnsian democracy was flexible, and could apply beyond the national community itself. The cost was ambiguity. Take 'Chains and slavery' in 'Scots wha hae...' and 'the coward slave' in 'A Man's a Man'. In Scotland in 1793 some men *were* slaves, a status defended by Fletcher of Saltoun with nationalistic arguments. Scots pressed for the end of black slavery, but benefited greatly from its products, the tobacco and cotton which commercialised the country. Had Burns settled in Jamaica in 1786 he would have been a part of this.

Even the triumph of 'liberal' economics was coupled with the rise of wage-slavery, conceived in Carlyle's 'cash-nexus', which influenced 19th-century social-critical literature and Marxism.

The result was that, as Scottish democracy consolidated, the wage-slave was defined in racial terms; with the Irish increasingly distrusted as racially inferior because prepared to tolerate the economic division of labour, providing a low-cost, though physically powerful labour force. Burns died before the

Irish rising of 1798. How would he have reacted to it? Probably as a presbyterian radical of the Henry Joy McCracken sort. Yet subsequently Ulster presbyterian radicalism was bribed out of existence. The part of Scotland he came from was deeply hostile to Catholicism, and Burns' freemasonry and popularity among Ulster Scots—who continued to quote the Declaration of Arbroath on their banners, but directed it against Dublin rather than London rule—reinforced their Protestant nationalism.

The Scottish attitude to France was quite different: the optimism of James Mackintosh's *Vindiciae Gallica* (1791) certainly gave way to Burkeian pessimism; but the revolution was regarded as inevitable in John Galt's *Annals of the Parish* (1820), followed by Carlyle's *French Revolution* (1837). Carlyle agreed with Burns that the French King was no tragic victim but someone whose indolence and stupidity only accelerated his inevitable downfall, much like the Stewarts. He passed this evolutionism on to Engels, typical enough of the radicals who universalised Burns (he liked to believe that his Irish partner, Mary Burns, was a kinswoman) while dismissing Scots exceptionality: an occluded vision that passed to a later generation of historians and literary scholars, from Christopher Hill to Raymond Williams, who established Marxism at he heart of the Anglo-British canon.

III AULD SCOTIA—WHO SHE?

What is lacking is national pathos, or more directly, sex: Scotia not only isn't Britannia, she does not seem to be there at all. Woman-as-nation can personify integrity—the national matron—along with dependence, martyrdom, and liability to rape. With the last comes miscegenation, an attack on ethnic purity. So she is both radical and conservative: Marianne and, alternatively, Marie Antoinette. Seamus Deane has cited Burke on the French Queen as the birth of anti-modern Irish nationalism. Eccentric? Paine was read far more than Burke in Ireland itself—yet Marianne/Marie Antoinette personify powerful if antithetical images of the nation: the fructifying mother and the symbol of traditional reverence. Both have roots in Catholic cults of the Madonna. Deane rightly sees this as critical: the nation as as aspect of Burke's sublime.

Burnsian patriotism has different roots: in the covenanted nature of the Scots state, and in its concurrence with the 'authoritarian family' of Emanuel Todd: the Scots family as a contractual, not an affective, unit, underwritten by male actors and main force. 'La Marseillaise's' nation is female, her subjects are her children; 'Wha for Scotland's king and law...' implies no such relationship. Its maleness is further emphasised by Wallace, castrated, beheaded and quartered, symbolically eradicating the Scottish nation. 'Scots wha hae' involves a rebirth, but the seed is the blood—and co-operation—of warriors. Women do not figure at all.

Scotswomen were, despite actually keeping society in existence, mistrusted. In recurrent witch-hunts social solidarity was bought through female sacrifice as the 'authoritarian families', whose various layers made up the state, turned on them as scapegoats when things did not work out. A later élite responded by engineering a sort of Smithian 'sympathy': adopting 'feeling' of the Henry Mackenzie sort, and incorporating female characteristics which also met certain conservative criteria. A more general status of victimhood could be conferred on Celtic monks slaughtered by the Norsemen, George Wishart and the Calvinist martyrs, and in the late seventeenth century the Covenanters. This was when Scotland's two images—Covenanter and Highlander—confronted each other; Whiggism and nationalism interwove and created extreme pyschological pressure. James Hogg seems to have been peculiarly alive to it, in 'The Brownie of Bodsbeck' (1815), with a psychological insight he learned from the pioneer psychoanalyst Professor Andrew Duncan. This got full play in *The Memoirs and Confessions of a Justified Sinner* (1823).

Sado-sexual themes, central to 'the romantic agony', have an uneasy presence in a nation dominated by sublimation and repression. In John Galt's *The Provost* (1821) a pretty, silly teenager is hanged for infanticide; Scott has the immurement of an adultress in *Marmion* (1808), fragile women persecuted in *The Heart of Midlothian* (1816) and *The Bride of Lammermoor* (1819). George Douglas Brown's *The House with the Green Shutters* (1901) ends up with the Gourlay women killing themselves to the accompaniment of I Corinthians 13, expressive of all that Victorian Scotland was not. Femininity—or sensitivity in general—became a sort of civic disqualification, to be overcome by becoming 'more like men'. This emotional inflexibility, latent in R D Laing's critique of the family, has had its Scottish roots analysed by Kay Carmichael in *For Crying out Loud* (1993)

What does one do in such circumstances? One answer was to re-engineer 'sympathy' to stress tactical victimhood, exile and loss, even by those who had success in commercial life. The ambitious young Scot Donald Farfrae performs this in Thomas Hardy's *The Mayor of Casterbridge* (1886):

The singer himself grew emotional, till she could imagine a tear in his eye as the words went on:—

'It's hame, and it's hame, hame fain would I be,
Oh hame, hame, hame to my ain countree!
There's an eye that ever weeps, and a fair face will be fain,
As I pass through Annan Water with my bonnie bands again;
When the flower is in the bud, and the leaf upon the tree,
The lark shall sing me hame to my ain countree!'

Young Farfrae repeated the last verse. It was plain that nothing so pathetic had been heard at the Three Mariners for a considerable time. The difference of accent, the excitability of the singer, the intense local feeling, and the seriousness with which he worked himself up to a climax, surprised this set of worthies, who were only too prone to shut up their emotions with caustic words.

It was to be in the 1880s that Scots expatriates, under pressure for sharp business practices and energetic colonial activity, were to bind themselves together in Burns Clubs and St Andrew or Caledonian Societies. R L Stevenson would give them yet more pabulum in *The Master of Ballantrae*. *En route* to the West Indies, and the novel's strange climax, the Master, Alexander Durie, trying to win over Ephraim McKellar, launches into 'the saddest of our country tunes, which sets folk weeping in a tavern':

Now, when the day dawns on the brow of the moorland,
Low stands the house, and the chimney-stone is cold.
Lone let it stand, now the folks are all departed,
The kind hearts, the true hearts, that loved the place of old.

The image is that of the Clearances—revived by the Scottish Land Leaguers—but the Master is a formidably confused character: he and his brother suffer not just from national history but from the proto-schizophrenia and degeneracy which, at the same time, Flaubert and Zola were diagnosing in French bourgeois society.

Allan Ramsay, Adam Smith and Henry Mackenzie, the psalmody of the Convenanters and the Jacobite songs, washed Scotland into tactical martyrdom by a combination of patriotism and sentiment. A sentimentalised Burns, Jacobite, radical and romantic, could revive nationality through song and a fetishised exile, blamed on remote landlords, religious rivals, the immigrant 'other'. Self-repression had to fight it out with false consciousness.

V FRUSTRATED LIBERATORS

This instrumental patriotism dispensed with the geographic loyalties of Hoffmann von Fallersleben's 'Deutschland, Deutschland über alles' (1841), otherwise very Burnsian in its addiction to wine, women and song, or the linguistic ones of the Parry brothers' 'Hen Wlad fy Nhadau' (Land of my Fathers) (1854) which stemmed from Welsh defence of their language against Anglo-Scottish education commissioners in 1848. The Scoto-imperial vision of T B Macaulay's 'Lays of Ancient Rome' (1842), as much as Samuel Smiles' *Self Help* (1859) carries on its spirit:

And how can man die better, than facing fearful odds,
For the ashes of his fathers and the temples of his Gods?

Derived in part from Carlyle's *Heroes and Hero-Worship* (1841), this was a calculating commitment to an Empire which was emphatically 'British', not English. The Bonnymuir Rebels of 1820, those cleared from the straths, the Free Kirkers who lost church and manse: through emigration and democracy in the colonies, these could transform their status from victim to elite. A century of success followed in which the superman—from Carlyle via Smiles' engineers to MacDiarmid's Lenin—was Scotland's version of the sublime.

But what happened when the momentum ebbed? Sir Robert Lorimer's Scottish National War Memorial was built in 1928 in Edinburgh Castle: not just commemorating soldiers killed in the War, but those mobilised to supply war and tend its casualties: miners, railwaymen, shipbuilders, women munitions workers and nurses. More than the systemic Cross of Sacrifice of the Imperial War Graves Commission, this was an epitaph for a society crippled by war which had still not recovered. Tom Johnston in his *History of the Working Class in Scotland* (1922) had already inverted the national or religious discourse, stressing exploitation and division: coal-owners against collier-serfs, cotton-magnates against spinners, engineering employers against shop stewards. Working-class solidarity dominates his fellow ILPer Hugh

MacDiarmid's 'Ballad of the General Strike', the central section of *A Drunk Man Looks at the Thistle* (1926). It also failed:

> A coward growth in that lorn stock
> That wrought the sorry trick?
> The thistle be a rocket soared
> And cam' doon like the stick

This 'heart of a heartless world' revived, not by renegotiating an inclusive Scots patriotism, but incubating national pathos as a distinctive but still overwhelmingly male sequence of victims: John MacLean, the Hunger Marchers, the Benny Lynches and John Thomsons, sporting heroes who died young; unsung inventors like Logie Baird.

MacDiarmid and Grassic Gibbon even managed to turn the left's frustration into something untouched by Burns—a religious epiphany: the cruxifixion imagery of 'The Ballad of the General Strike' in the *Drunk Man*, the plea of the Good Thief: 'Lord, Remember me, when thou enterest thy kingdom' of *Cloud Howe*. This played on the Covenanting past; the Clydesider MPs were seen off south in 1922 by the singing of Psalm 124:

> Then Israel may say, and that truly
> If that the Lord had not our cause maintained
> When cruel men against us furiously
> Rose up in wrath to make of us their prey…

This fused national and class consciousness, and provided a martyr, John MacLean, whose memory was reworked by nationalists and socialists into the vigorous socialist patriotism of Hamish Henderson's anthems:

> When MacLean meets wi' freens in Springburn
> A' the roses an' geans 'll turn tae bloom,
> An' the black boy frae 'yont Nyanga
> Dings the fell gallows o' the burghers doon.

But the route out after 1926, for both Gibbon and (less successfully) MacDiarmid involved a British socialism: a High Road to London, shared with another inconvenient man of the Celtic left, Sean O'Casey, when he broke with Yeats over the Abbey Theatre's rejection of *The Silver Tassie* in

1928. The Burnsian note is somehow appropriate. Their battle was shrill, bloody and fought out down south.

It echoed a situation where industry remained but control was surrendered. Shipping, banks and railways went after World War I, then the heavy industries, with nationalisation and depression in the 1950s and 1960s. Light industry, oil and electronics were from the beginning controlled from abroad; financial services might have originated among successful Scottish capitalists, but were effectively a form of tax avoidance remote from building up the Scots manufacturing economy. The absence of a Scottish state exacerbated this—Tom Nairn's 'river of loss' reverses, with good reason, Sir Walter Scott's great metaphor of the Union as the vitalisation of historical inevitability— though an anticipation of the negative element marks Scott's late work *The Chronicles of the Canongate* (1827).

The road not taken was emphatic enough. Victimhood—the soldiers of the Fifth Army in Italy, the 'D-Day Dodgers', symbolically purging imperial misdeeds—is overcome in Hamish Henderson's 'Freedom Come all Ye' (1950): its inclusive, socialist, anti-racialist discourse gives legitimacy to Scotland as a civic nationality, with the pedigree of the European city states behind it, back to Macaulay's republican Rome. But this meant restoring the old quasi-Marxian scale of values—of progress or economic development or ecology— which subverts the centrality of the nation, or blends it with other centres of authority.

VI POST-INDUSTRIAL PATRIOTISM

The space between victim and tragic hero, and victim and loser is narrow. By rejecting the Philoctetic stance, 'improving' Scots set out to beat the dominant partner at its own game. But what if the British bourgeois state loses its own solidarity? Globalisation in general and the European Union in particular, have incubated a victim cult within *England* itself: 'This is John, he moans for Middle England' as a *Times* cartoon cleverly put it. The 'campaign for the countryside', the 'recreational mourning' when Diana, Princess of Wales died, even the premier's 'scars on my back' when his market reforms were frustrated, had almost precise parallels with bad old Scots traditions.

MacLeanism remained the left's response, but by the time devolution arrived, its power had evaporated. If globalisation and deindustrialisation hit Scotland hard, 'the black boy frae 'yont Nyanga' was hit even harder under an ANC government whose socialism promptly surrendered to the IMF.

Kelman's 'It will be horror' reflects the end of the solidarity of workmates and trade unionists, where 'victimless change' can destroy Ravenscraig, and Scottish Enterprise seduce investors by promising 'satisfyingly low' wages. This 'excluded Scotland', the land of drugs and violence, would be reinforced by the 'winners' in Gleneagles and Skibo.

At this point citizenship decays into the sentiment of 'a land that is lost now'. In *Braveheart* it is being outbred by the enemy, in this case English, but arguably in Redneck America non-caucasian. The threats to Kelman's 'excluded Scotland' shift from authoritarian/capitalist to the junkie or jobless, violent youth. These can be inverted: in the Brian Souter/Cardinal Winning 'Keep the Clause' campaign a capitalist and a conservative clergyman convinced at least a majority of Scottish tabloid-readers that they and their vulnerable children were the prospective victims of homosexual perverts. Many more were at risk from their own families.

One mode of avoiding Philoctetic victimhood is to ironise it. Cue the Tartan Army. It began quasi-millenial in 1977: devolution stood on the runway, the Scots were oil sheikhs *in spe*, and even beat England at Wembley, creating a *grand peur* in North London. The Scots went to Argentina to win the World Cup, and 'Ally's Tartan Army' was born. The débàcle of 1978—defeat by Peru, victory over finalist Holland—didn't just show that strategy was not one of the nation's finer points, it made the relation of the supporters to the team semi-detached; a politics which identified England supporters as thuggish quasi-fascists while the Scots' ludic posturings eventually changed the culture of the World Cup contests held in France. Football-supporting became carnivalesque and consequently utterly remote from Calvinism, with the Scots as the '*Narren*': a ritual of excess and purgation—essentially from Catholic tradition—replaced the hubris of Calvinism. A people as unhealthy as the Scots blew its chance of sporting success anyway. But ludic Scotland also replaced the immanent tragedy of overreach with a parody: the hirsute patriots of *Braveheart* became the Army in their 'Jimmie Hats', largely from unthreatening (if not actually servile) jobs in the service industries.

Irony has limits: sport-capitalism will stop the Tartan Army wandering the world in support of mediocre football teams. The hangover can take the form of Kelman's Beckettian *stasis* , the life-threatening diet of Inspector Rebus, or of the commercial self-disgust of Irvine Welsh:

A place ay dispossessed white trash in a trash country fill ay dispossessed white trash. Some say that the Irish are the trash ay Europe. That's shite.

34

It's the Scots. The Irish hud the bottle tae win thir country back, or at least maist ay it. Ah remember getting wound up when Nicksy's brar, down in London, described the Scots as 'porridge wogs'. Now ah realise that the only thing offensive about that statement was its racism against black people. Otherwise it's spot-on. Anybody will tell you; the Scots make good soldiers. Like ma brar, Billy.

At the cusp of the millennium, the outcome is not promising. The extreme centralisation of Blairite unionism is not matched by the investment of the Scots political class in the state: not just parliament but the necessary institutions of civil society. These are now, anyway, regarded elsewhere as *démodé*. As the 'voluntary sacrifice' of liberal nationalism becomes a necessity, it fails to fit into a hyperindividualism whose allegiance is to commodities: designer clothes, fast food, alcohol, drugs. The Scots' problem is that this commodity world, banging up against the partially-reconstituted nation, may be one disruption too many.

From David Stewart to Andy Stewart: the Invention and Re-invention of the Scottish Soldier

Trevor Royle

Back in 1961 when the British public was trying to make up its mind whether it preferred Elvis Presley or Helen Shapiro the popular music charts were infiltrated by a curiously cod song called 'The Scottish Soldier' performed by an equally cod singer called Andy Stewart. Although it never made number one the song stayed in the charts for forty weeks and with its catchy words and robust tune it enjoyed a wide currency, not just in Scotland and the rest of the United Kingdom but in most parts of the English-speaking world.

Stewart, an entertainer in the mould of Harry Lauder, was equally popular. Born in Arbroath—he was listed as one the town's tourist attractions alongside the Declaration—he had come to the fore as a jaunty leading performer on the BBC's White Heather Club, an all-singing and all-dancing programme of light entertainment which provided a sanitised version of the traditional ceildih. The men wore kilts with sensible shirts and ties, the women wore white dresses with sashes and set-piece dances such as 'The Duke of Perth' and 'Hamilton House' were danced with formal precision to music provided by the accordion-led bands of Jimmy Shand or Bobby Macleod.

The songs were equally well crafted and were sung with gusto by Stewart and other performers such as James Urquhart. Many were traditional songs sung to strictly modulated tunes; others were adapted or in the case of 'The Scottish Soldier' given contrived words. The tune of this particular song was a march called 'The Green Hills of Tyrol' which dates back to the Crimean War of 1854-1856. The Highland Brigade served alongside units from the Sardinian army whose bands played a similar march adapted from the music of Rossini and it was re-adapted again for the pipes and drums. 'The Green Hills of Tyrol' became a regular feature in the repertoire of the pipes and drums of most of Scotland's infantry regiments—both the Black Watch and the Argyll and Sutherland Highlanders still list it as a Retreat air in their list of duty tunes—but the words gave the medley its poignancy. The soldier 'with good broad shoulder' tells the story of 'battles glorious and deeds victorious' but far away from home and, with death close at hand, 'he's sighing, his heart is crying' and he longs to leave 'these green foreign hills' because they are 'not the hills of home'.

This was sentimentality run riot. Of course, that was part of the appeal and Stewart milked it in such a way that in his kilt he became the personification of all the manliness embodied in the figure of the Scottish soldier. His audience fell for the illusion too and found themselves being caught up in the stirring three-four march tune and the associated heroism of words that could have come from the pen of Sir Walter Scott or William Edmonstoune Aytoun.

And now this soldier, this Scottish soldier,
Who wanders far no more, and soldiers far no more,
Now on a hillside, a Scottish hillside,
You'll see a piper play this soldier home.
He's seen the glory, he's told the story,
Of battles glorious, and deeds victorious;
But he will cease now, he is at peace now,
Far from these green hills of Tyrol.

In 1961 the Scottish soldier was still a potent figure in the country's iconography and Stewart's song was very much at one with the spirit of the times. Although defence cuts had removed the names of the Highland Light Infantry, the Royal Scots Fusiliers and the Cameron and Seaforth Highlanders (all lost to amalgamation) the army still had in its order of battle eight Scottish line infantry regiments, two battalions of Scots Guards and one armoured regiment, the Royal Scots Greys. Scots made up 13% of the army's personnel and with National Service still in being—the last conscript was not demobbed until May 1963—kilted soldiers were a common sight in public places and would remain so until the following decade when the Troubles in Northern Ireland put a stop to military personnel wearing uniform off-duty. The relationship between the public and the kilted Jock was not just illusion. In 1968 the Argyll and Sutherland Highlanders were faced with disbandment, partly as a result of further defence cuts and partly (it was widely thought) as a result of their robust approach in dealing with the insurrection in Aden prior to the British withdrawal and transfer of power three years earlier. The Argylls were not the only victims of the cuts. The Cameronians, a Lowland regiment with an older history and lineage, were also earmarked for disbandment, a decision the regiment accepted with commendable dignity, but a well organised and noisy campaign was begun by the Highland regiment's supporters to 'Save the Argylls'. Over a million signatures were collected for a petition which was presented to parliament and although some Labour MPs, notably Barbara Castle and Tam Dalyell, criticised the regiment for alleged heavy-handedness during the Aden operation the Argylls were saved. In 1970 it was announced that it would remain on the army's Order of Battle in company strength—some 120 men—and a year later it was quietly restored as a full battalion, perversely as a result of the need to garrison Northern Ireland.

All this mattered to the people of Scotland. The campaign was rarely off the front pages of the nation's press, its colourful diced Balmoral cap logo was seen everywhere and in 1968, a year when revolution gripped Europe, saving the Argylls became the most widely discussed political topic in Scotland. At a time when devolution was still an impossible dream—the former SNP leader Arthur Donaldson told his successor Billy Wolfe that 'all the activists of the SNP could have been the complement on a small passenger aircraft, and had they flown together and crashed without survivors, the cause of independence would have been lost to view for many years'—the kilted Scottish soldier became a handy substitute. Indeed the campaigners recognised that deep-rooted sentiment, and their cause was not hindered by the success of the SNP in 1967 when Winnie Hamilton won the Hamilton by-election and in 1968 the party won control of Cumbernauld. Never mind that SNP activists campaigned against the presence of the Polaris nuclear bases on the Clyde and adopted an anti-militarist stance which still divides the party four decades later; the campaigners for the Argylls recognised the potency of the Scottish military connection and played on it. In their view anyone who loved Scotland wanted to save the Argylls.

In fact the love affair between the Scots and their soldiers was already long established. During the First World War the Scots provided more recruits per head of population than any other part of the United Kingdom and the casualties were correspondingly high—some 100,000 or 13% of the British total, most of them infantry privates. Their reasons why they swarmed into uniform are varied and defy a simple explanation. Partly it was a result of the general enthusiasm for war, the patriotic rush of 1914 which saw the creation of a huge volunteer army, and in that respect a sense of adventure also played a part. In Glasgow alone twenty thousand had volunteered by the end of August and in the following year two battalions of the Highland Light Infantry, the local regiment, had been formed exclusively from men who worked in the corporation's tramways department or were members of the Boys' Brigade. Partly it was patriotism, suffused in many cases by peer pressure or threats from above—one landowner, the Earl of Wemyss, gave notice that every able-bodied man aged between 18 and 30 working on his estates would be put on half-pay for the duration of the war, and their jobs kept open, provided they joined up. 'If they do not enlist,' continued the Earl's offer, 'they will be compelled to leave my employment.'

A further reason was provided by recent history and the creation of dubious traditions. In the middle of the previous century Scotland had been gripped by the Volunteer craze, that Victorian fancy for part-time amateur soldiering which involved some gentle shooting practice and drills and, best of all, dressing up in turkey-cock uniforms. In Scotland the recruitment figures for the Volunteer units were twice the UK average, a figure which was undoubtedly assisted by the creation of units with Highland affiliations, most of them in the central belt. With their panoply of kilts, tartan trews, ostrich feathers, ornate sporrans and pipe bands they were an irresistible attraction and everywhere men rushed to wear them. Most of these outlandish uniforms owed nothing to tradition but were invented by local colonels and they came to represent self-conscious nationalism or what the military historian John Keegan has described as 'a force for resistance against the creeping anglicisation of Scottish urban life.' (1) Nostalgia for a half-forgotten romantic past was a factor, as was the existing iconography of the Scottish soldier ('a lion in the field, a lamb in the house'), which found its apotheosis in Roger Fenton's Crimean War photographs of the sternly bearded Highland soldiers of Queen Victoria's army. However, there was more to soldiering than putting on fancy dress. Being a part-time soldier meant following an honourable calling: it was companionable, offered self-respect and produced steadiness of character, all important moral virtues in Presbyterian Scotland.

From being a feared figure, no better than a savage in the badlands north of the Highland Line, the Highlander was reborn as an entirely admirable character and his dress, a much despised dull checked cloth, was transformed into confections based on a colourful and carefully codified set of tartans, most of them created with unhistorical abandon. Even the regiments were given their own contrived tartans and added further adornments, buckles and badges to produce a military fashion which would have been unrecognised by any soldier who had fought under Montrose and Alasdair MacColla or Charles Edward Stewart and Lord George Murray. The reasons for this transformation have been much studied and the phenomenon, known variously as tartan kitsch or Balmorality, has been subjected to hostile analysis, so much so that the political commentator Andrew Marr was moved to remark that 'the deconstruction of the tartan cult is in danger of itself becoming a cult.' (2)

The vogue can also be traced back to the defeat of the Jacobite army at Culloden in 1746 and to the subsequent subjugation of the Highlands and the despoliation of its Gaelic culture. The destruction of Highland Scottish military power and the Clearances of the traditional clan lands have been described as the beginning of the end of a way of life which was barely understood by outsiders, not least Lowland Scots, and it has to be said that, at the time, the process was largely welcomed. In the aftermath of the union of the parliaments and the economic benefits of 'heavenly Hanoverianism' it was thought no bad thing to have this lawless area with its savage population and their heathen way of life (for so it seemed) brought under control. What to do with them was another matter. Either they could accept modernity and the union or they could be moved elsewhere to make new lives, courtesy of landowners who regarded themselves not as destroyers but as liberal reformers. As for the soldierly instincts of their tenants, these could be offered to the British Army at a time when it was being used as an imperial gendarmerie to expand the country's growing colonial holdings. Or as Winston Churchill neatly summarised the outcome: 'Pitt canalised the martial ardour of the Highlanders into the service of his Imperial dreams.' (3)

With the barbaric allure of their uniforms Scottish soldiers became an instantly recognised and widely feared element of the British Army and their service in Africa, India and north America helped to consolidate Britain's growing mercantile empire. Many individuals enriched themselves in the process and the history of the eighteenth century conquest of India is littered with examples of rapacious Scots making fortunes for themselves while serving in the army of the East India Company and returning home as wealthy 'nabobs'. As Victor Kiernan put it in his essay 'Scottish Soldiers and the Conquest of India' the Victorian tendency to romanticise the kilted Highlander had to be balanced by the reality behind his creation—'the harm done to Scotland was deeper than any matter of antiquarian externals; it must be measured against the harm done by Scots, in the course of their junior partnership with England in the pursuit of imperial wealth.' (4) They might have been gallant soldiers but when they left Scotland many left behind their consciences, leaving the poet Thomas Campbell to lament of their actions:

Rich in the gems of India's gaudy zone,
And plunder piled from kingdoms not their own,
Degenerate trade! thy minions could despise
The heartborn anguish of a thousand cries . . .
(from 'The Pleasures of Hope')

Campbell's complaint can be given substance by many examples, none better than the Scottish entrepreneur John Johnstone of Westerhall who made a fortune in India second only to Robert Clive's, but it is not the whole story. The Highland soldiers who served in America and Canada played a similar role to the Hessian forces which served in the same campaigns against the French and native Americans and in that sense they were just as much mercenaries as the Scots who used the East India Company as a kind of latter-day French Foreign Legion. In that sense too they were following an even older tradition—that of the mercenaries who served in French, Swedish or Spanish service during the Thirty Years War. To them war was a lucrative national industry which had the added bonus that it could be exported.

Scots made good fighters and in common with many other minorities on Europe's fringes—the Croat cavalry in Wallenstein's army, for example—they exported their skills to the highest bidder, becoming soldiers of fortune who gave good value for money. At least 25,000 were in the service of Gustavus Adolphus of Sweden, half as many fought for King Louis XIII of France, often confronting their fellow countrymen on the field of battle, neither giving quarter nor expecting to receive it. One, Sir John Hepburn, scion of an old East Lothian Catholic family, fought in the Swedish and the French armies and rose to become a Marshal of France, having raised the formation which lives on today as The Royal Scots, the 1st of Foot and the senior line infantry regiment in the British Army's order of battle. Yet, despite his aristocratic antecedents he too knew his price. Trusted as one of the bravest of Gustavus's brigade commanders Hepburn lost his patron's confidence prior to the Battle of Lützen which saw the Swedish king lose his life in 1632 and had departed his camp with the reproachful words: 'And now sire never more shall this sword be drawn in your service; this is the last time I will ever serve so ungrateful a prince!' Men like Hepburn or other notables such Alexander Leslie who commanded the parliamentary forces at Marston Moor in 1644 during the Wars of the Three Kingdoms all learned the soldiers' trade fighting as soldiers of fortune and it is one of the ironies of Andy Stewart's song that his Scottish soldier is in reality a mercenary and not one of the kilted heroes of later years.

However the history of the Scots as mercenaries does not altogether explain the reason why Scotland swallowed the myth of the Scottish soldier. Their exploits took place many miles away and while they were a matter for pride they were only one of many components of the nation's increasingly confused identity during the eighteenth and nineteenth centuries. In any case many of the soldiers in the Scottish regiments, as in other regiments, were Irish. In 1838 the strength of the army was 89,000, 40% of whom were Irish and only 12% were Scots. By then they were British soldiers in British regiments with only the Highland regiments wearing kilts and dressing themselves in tartan while Lowland units such as the Royal Scots wore the regulation red tunic and the other appurtenances of line infantry regiment. It would take a king's visit and a quarrel between two Highland historians to change all that.

The monarch was King George IV and the rivals were Sir David Stewart of Garth and Alasdair Ranaldson, MacDonnell of Glengarry. The king's visit to Edinburgh in August 1822 was the first to be made by a British monarch since 1651 when Charles II left the country with his Scottish army to try to win back his throne in return for imposing Presbyterianism on his three kingdoms. The attempt ended in ignominy at Worcester and Charles went into exile. On his restoration to the throne in 1660 he never visited his northern kingdom again, the memory of his last residence there being too painful—the long sermons in Falkland Palace, the brow-beating by Covenanting divines and as Bishop Gilbert Burnet remembered the strict regime: 'if at any time there had been gaiety at court, such as dancing or playing at cards, he [Charles] was severely reproved for it.' In the intervening 171 years no British monarch had troubled themselves to visit Scotland and perhaps with good reason; in that time the Stewarts made two attempts to retrieve their thrones from the House of Hanover and the parliament of Scotland was united with that of England in 1707.

By the end of the eighteenth century the country was becoming urbanised and with heavy industry taking root in the Forth and Clyde valleys its population was centred mainly in the central belt. The long retreat from the countryside had begun, a process hastened by improving landlords who were destroying the old ties that bound their tenants to the land by removing them and making way for modern agrarian methods in the name of commercial development. All over the country, but especially in the Highlands, people were moved off land to make way for sheep and cattle; in the first instances they were settled on the coastal areas but later they were forced to emigrate, mainly to north America. For the rural population this was the end of an old way of life: not having security of tenure they had no voice in the matter and, as Tom Devine puts it, 'the old social order was destroyed for ever.' (5)

Paradoxically, it was at this juncture that sentiment got the better of reality. At the very moment that a way of life was disappearing many of the men responsible for the loss began forming themselves into societies to celebrate the Highlands and Gaelic culture and society. Most were utterly bogus, drawing on instant traditions which allowed the membership to dress up in tartan fancy-dress, dance reels and strathspeys, drink copious amounts of whisky and make sentimental toasts to the grandeur of dear old Scotia. As social gatherings they were harmless enough but the members took their duties solemnly and became arbiters of taste, the Highland Society of London quickly assuming predominance in such matters, haughtily rebuking lesser souls for wearing the wrong button with the right tartan. Naturally this led to altercations which were fiercely debated, friends fell out over points of precedence and dress as the different groups attempted to codify and reinvent the past. One example will stand for many. Here is a description of the annual ball of the Society of True Highlanders, penned in 1816 by its founder Glengarry, a man of uncertain temper who was best known for single-handedly manufacturing the traditions and life-style of a Highland chieftain and for forcing his tenants off the clan lands.

The guests almost to a man were in the full uniform of their regiments or the Garb of Old Gaul [tartan and kilts], and such a scene of enthusiastic and harmonious enjoyment was not perhaps to be instanced, and quite beyond description; the richer dresses of the ladies were superbly appropriate, and among the Highland costumes some were mounted with the ancient clasps of Siol Chinn in gold and silver, or hereditary buttons bearing the heads of all the Kings and Queens of Scotland. Colonel Stewart of Garth wore large round cairngorm buttons richly set. Others had the globular silver buttons of their ancestry, and the richly-finished pistols, dirks, powder-horns and other paraphernalia of the rich Milesian costume gave an air or magnificence to the whole, far more brilliant than expectation had sanctioned at their first fete. (6)

This is just plain silly but the *Inverness Journal* of the day published it unblushingly along with many other equally ridiculous and fanciful accounts and Glengarry was proud of his efforts at promoting a way of life which had no basis in fact. The mention of David Stewart of Garth's name is interesting for at the time both men were united in their efforts to rewrite Highland history and to celebrate the Gaelic way of life. They might have remained on friendly terms, too, but for George IV's visit when the responsibility for organising the 'plaided panorama' which accompanied it fell not to Glengarry's True Highlanders but to Stewart of Garth's rival Celtic Society of Edinburgh. Edinburgh went tartan-mad during the ten days that George IV graced the capital and under the direction of the novelist Sir Walter Scott who acted as pageant-master an invented mythology of Highland customs, replete with clan gatherings and balls, was represented as solid historical fact. The story of the bitter quarrel between the two antiquarians is a minor episode in John Prebble's sardonic account of the visit, *The King's Jaunt*, and sorry reading it makes too as both men sought to gain the sartorial high ground about matters to do with the belted plaid and the shoulder plaid and the correct way to wear tartan dress.

Stewart of Garth was preferred as the arbiter of Highland taste mainly because he enjoyed Scott's confidence but also because he had just published his *Sketches of the Character, Manner and Present State of the Highlanders of Scotland, with Details of the Military Service of the Highland Regiments*. So successful had it been that three editions were published in quick succession and it laid the foundations on which all other Highland military histories have been created. Most of Stewart of Garth's soldiering had been done in the 42nd Highlanders, better known as the Black Watch. His original intention had been to write his regiment's history, its records having been lost while campaigning in France and Flanders, but as he had to put that history in context the work was extended to include a more general military history of the Highland regiments. The end result was a compelling and largely accurate account.

It was also compassionately written not least because Stewart of Garth believed that the way of life of his beloved Highlanders was under threat from rapacious landowners and that unless their shameless behaviour was stopped 'the high-spirited, faithful affectionate Highlanders will become envious, unprincipled, ferocious Irishmen.' While there was a fair degree of paternalism in Stewart of Garth's treatment of the Highlanders he proved to be an unstinting critic of the landowners and clan chiefs who were extirpating their people for financial gain. Amongst the worst of the offenders was Glengarry whom Stewart of Garth castigated for ousting his tenants while masquerading as a kilted and plaided Highland chief. In a letter to his friend Sir John Macgregor Murray of Lanrick he complained that while Glengarry paraded his deep feelings for his fellow countrymen of 1500 souls who once worked his farms only 35 remained. 'Who has done more to extirpate the race so far as his power extended?' he asked.

Unfortunately, Murray of Lanrick and others persuaded the author to tone down his criticism of Highland landowners. Although reproachful words are present in the *Sketches* Prebble believes that the original manuscript, now lost, contained a less mild mannered attack than appeared in the published version and that pressure had been put on the author to restrain his language. 'Even so,' concludes Prebble, 'it was startling in its argument and its attack, and wrapped as these were in a readable history of the Highland regiments, they ensured the initial success of the book.' (7) If that had been that, if the book had appeared without George IV venturing on his jaunt to Edinburgh, Stewart of Garth might have had a different kind of reputation. Instead of being remembered as a serious historian and a writer who was prepared to criticise Highland landlords—no easy thing to do at a time when the weavers' Radical Insurrection had taken place only two years previously and there was widespread fear of a workers' revolt—his name is better known for his association with the absurd pageantry surrounding the king's visit. It was Stewart of Garth who organised the parade of Highlanders which set the seal on the ceremonial, Scott's 'great gathering of the Gael' or 'the tartan confederacy' in which clan chiefs rode or marched in triumph from Holyroodhouse to Edinburgh Castle and, despite his misgivings, it was he who connived in creating the whole Celtic fantasy.

Innocuous in itself—the Duke of Atholl dismissed George IV's jaunt as a fortnight of play-acting—the visit left a hangover from which Scotland never fully recovered. It cemented the kilt as the national dress and created a bogus tartan caricature which became the accepted and increasingly acceptable face of Scotland. The Royal Family became part of the myth and after George's porcine figure had appeared swathed in tartan successive kings and princes have lost no opportunity to don the kilt when in Scotland. For a country whose identity was increasingly bound up with its English neighbour and a time of encroaching anglicisation of Scottish life tartan kilts and an imagined Highland past became a means of satisfying a deep emotional need. From being bare-arsed bandits, the scourge of the Lowlands and a figure which created equal amounts of fun and fear the Highlander was transformed utterly into a manly, colourful, patriotic figure who managed to be both respected and respectable. And in no other part of Scottish life, did this put down deeper roots than in its regiments. Once derided, the figure of the Scottish soldier became an admired exemplar, stern in his kilts and plaids and ostrich feathers and unbending in his patriotic duty to country and empire. By the century's end even the Lowland regiments were sporting tartan trews, Highland doublets and their officers carried basket-hilted claymores, a transformation which bemused military historians: 'They lacked only the kilt and feather bonnet to resemble the sort of figure whose ancestors their ancestors had despised, feared and slaughtered but who, by 1881, had come to personify Scotland.' (8)

Stewart died a disappointed man. Attacked unceasingly by Glengarry after the event he resumed his military career and died of fever in St Lucia in 1829 while serving as the colony's governor-general. Glengarry predeceased him a year earlier and with him died the Society of True Highlanders but he achieved a curious immortality. His portrait was painted by Henry Raeburn and bedecked in tartan it became one of Scotland's great Victorian icons, providing an image which was eagerly taken up by the manufacturers of whisky, shortbread and other nicknacks. For them and their products it said Scotland in a way that few other symbols could and had not Raeburn executed the portrait it would have been difficult to provide a substitute. The same thing can be said of the Scottish soldier: in his kilt and sporran, his feathered bonnet and white spats he is a colourful yet utterly respectable figure; marching in serried ranks behind the pipes and drums against the dramatic backcloth of Edinburgh or Stirling castle he is as familiarly Caledonian as the bonnie banks of Loch Lomond or the heather-covered Road to the Isles. As Prebble put it so witheringly in summing up Glengarry's and Stewart of Garth's legacy: 'No other nation has cherished so absurd an image, and none perhaps would accept it while knowing it to be a lie.' (9)

Notes

1. John Keegan, *Six Armies in Normandy* (London, 198), 168
2. Andrew Marr, *The Battle for Scotland* (London, 1992), 28
3. Winston S. Churchill, *A History of the English Speaking Peoples: The Age of Revolution*, vol 3 (London, 1957), 112
4. Victor Kiernan, 'Scottish Soldiers and the Conquest of India', in Grant S. Simpson (ed.), *The Scottish Soldier Abroad 1247-1967* (Edinburgh, 1992), 08
5. T. M. Devine, *The Scottish Nation 1700-2000* (London, 1999), 178
6. Account of True Highlanders' Ball in the *Inverness Journal*, in John Prebble, *The King's Jaunt: George IV in Scotland, August 1822* (London, 1988), 115
7. Prebble, 33-43
8. Stephen Wood, *The Scottish Soldier* (Manchester, 1987), 76
9. Prebble, p. 364

Hume, Sir James Frazer, Irony and Belief

Robert Fraser

Among the far-reaching elements of the Knoxian inheritance has been a conception of a national community defining itself less through works than faith, less through action than belief. Faith as an exclusive and defining force fuelled the Scottish Reformation; in the seventeenth century it inspired the Covenanters in their rebellion against Stewart—or Stuart—authority. In the eighteenth century a reaction set in, giving rise to a rational probing characteristic of the Scottish Enlightenment. In the nineteenth a related development took place, as reason turned on faith itself. One result was the splitting of the cultural psyche evidenced in James Hogg's *The Private Memoirs and Confessions of a Justified Sinner* and much of the fiction of Stevenson, as analysed superbly by Karl Miller in 1985 in his book *Doubles*. A second was a concerted interest in the theoretical underpinnings of all belief, that ranged well beyond Calvinism, and way beyond Scotland.

From the perspective of the Enlightenment the classic passage occurs towards the close of the chapter 'Of Miracles' from David Hume's *An Inquiry Concerning the Human Understanding* (1748). Hume has been considering the persistence of a belief in providential suspensions of the natural order. 'Our most holy religion,' he declares, 'is founded on faith, not on reason; and it is a sure method of exposing it to put it to a test that it is by no means fitted to endure'. He ends:

So that, upon the whole, we may conclude that the Christian religion not only was at first attended by miracles, but even at this day cannot be believed by any reasonable person without one. Mere reason is insufficient to convince us of its veracity. And whoever is moved by faith to assent to it is conscious of a continued miracle in his own person which subverts all the principles of his understanding and gives him a determination to believe what is most customary to custom and experience.

The balance of tone here is faultless, since it is impossible to infer without external evidence whether the sanctity imputed by Hume to 'our most holy religion' is the expression of residual reverence, even betting or tact. Hume's wit is ironical, but in a very particular mould. It consists of apparently taking the convictions proposed at face value, demonstrating their fallibility—or perhaps vulgarity—through the tenacity of surface logic. The demeanour does not slip: here is no grimace of vindication, even of mirth. The prose, the pose, is as deliberate as it is dour.

A century and a half later, and in England, the Glaswegian anthropologist Sir James Frazer wrote the following sentences in his chapter 'Oriental Religions in the West' from Part Four of the Third Edition of his comparative study of magic and religion, *The Golden Bough*. He has been discussing the coincidence in date during the later Roman Empire between Easter and the feast of the resurrection of Phrygian deity Attis. The Attis festival was older, and its adherents were thus inclined to claim that the Christian festival was based on it. Frazer comments:

This feeble argument the Christians easily rebutted. They admitted that in point of time Christ was the junior deity. But they triumphantly demonstrated his real seniority by falling back on the subtlety of Satan, who on so important an occasion had surpassed himself by inverting the usual order of nature.

Frazer's kinship with Hume is easy to discern. Both writers close with normality—that is with natural law—and both pretend to a respect for violations against it. A fine sense of philosophical history may detect the fact that Hume's 'custom and experience' and Frazer's 'usual order of nature' do not possess quite the same ring. Hume's experience is the result of cumulative judgement; it possesses no binding logical, or even empirical, force. Frazer by contrast is a late Victorian rather than an Enlightenment thinker: over matters of normality he is—or at least seems to be—more certain of his ground. In both men, however, clarity and humour present themselves in the form of a subversive and cutting dolorousness.

When Frazer read the works of his countryman Hume is not known. Presumably it was in the 1850s whilst an undergraduate at Glasgow. *The Treatise of Human Nature*, which had been widely dismissed on its first appearance a century before, had by the mid-nineteenth century become a set book in courses on metaphysics and epistemology in most Scottish universities. In its first volume Frazer would have read of the ubiquity and power of belief as a quality of the human mind, driving all cognitive systems. Hume's conclusions extend to the zone of faith, but their principal *exemplum* is the field of natural inference. The difference between reasonable and unreasonable belief is the number of instances, the stock of experience, shoring judgment up. Effects regularly followed causes, thus giving rise to rational convictions; miracles by definition happen infrequently and are therefore incredible. This sure-footed though subtle distinction much influenced Frazer, who was inclined to think of religion and magic as possessing the same logical structure as science, though resting on weaker foundations. Miraculous events as such could never emphatically be denied. All that could be done was to mock, gently to castigate, their insubstantiality. The mode of such derision was Frazerian irony.

The kinship with Hume goes further. As countless commentators have noted, Frazer's sub-classification of magic in his first part of his great work, *The Magic Art and the Evolution of Kings*, is derived directly from Hume's tabulation of the 'association of ideas', the network of conception that underlay notions of cause and effect. Just as Hume divides his association of ideas into connections of contiguity and resemblance, so Frazer parts magic into 'contagious' and 'sympathetic' kinds, the former exemplified by operating malevolently upon a victim's hair or nails, the latter by sticking a pin into a doll representing his person. Both pairs gave rise to conclusions that could not be demonstrated deductively, but which in the eyes of the believer were conclusive and effective. Magic and science thus reposed on common mental bedrock, the superiority of the latter over the former being a matter of reliability, and of that only. This contention had a tendency to undermine science, or as Hume would have called it natural philosophy. For Frazer it also boosted magic, which though obsolete was based on observation and intervention. 'After all,' as he carefully puts it, 'what we call truth is only the hypothesis which is found to work the best.' The challenge that this recognition posed to the contemporary mind recommended itself, both to his wit and to his intelligence.

Like Hume, moreover, Frazer was a sceptic rather than a dogmatic rationalist. Both men respected feeling, Hume as a forerunner of the Romantics, Frazer as their heir. Both felt subjective impressions to be dangerous and fallible; they also knew mankind to be powerless without them. In the first decade of the twentieth century Frazer became fascinated by the paradoxical play beneath this partial contradiction. Half of his mind, perhaps the better half, regarded magic, like religious practices and ideas, to be absurd. Like his anthropological predecessor Edward Burnett Taylor, it thought of such things as 'survivals' from an early stage of man's cultural development, 'standing over' from past ages, hence superstitions. A broader grasp of the historical canvas, however, could not but inform Frazer how pervasive such conventions were, and how useful. In this he was like Edward Gibbon, another Enlightenment forebear, who believed the Catholic monastic system, ridiculous in itself, to have carried Europe across the abyss of the Dark Ages. It is no accident that, in discussing related issues, Frazer's prose frequently takes on a Gibbonian weight and tone.

Modern marriage for example, the much-married Frazer maintained, was based on worn-out notions of exogamy and taboo, whilst property—that mainstay of capitalist society—was embroiled with dark awe of the totem. Yet these atavistic institutions stabilised the world, and enhanced human well-being. In 1909 Frazer delivered a lecture entitled 'Psyche's Task' at the Royal Institution in London, in which he cast himself in the role of a gowned 'devil's advocate'. His client was false belief which, Frazer pleaded, was 'a reed, a broken reed, which has yet supported the steps of many an erring brother, who might have stumbled and fallen. It is a light, a dim and wavering light, which, if it has lured many a mariner on the breakers, has yet guided some wanderers on life's troubled sea into a haven of rest and peace.' By implication we need occasionally to adhere to what we know to be untrue; abandoning such false convictions wholesale may lead to moral and social chaos.

The binding factor in this argument, I think, is the force of unreflecting habit. An habitual scholar, Frazer could not but be aware that mere habit represents a betrayal—or at least relaxation—of conscious thought. Habit, nonetheless, is what sustains our daily affairs by and large, and it is what kept

51

Frazer himself at the scholarly grindstone eighteen hours a day. Invention designed the Forth bridge, but habit is what built it. The Industrial Revolution consisted of vast Humean chains of cause and effect, effect and cause, each link a habit based on unthinking repetition. This, as Frazer was well aware, is the basis of mankind's social stability. As Henri Bergson was later to suggest in *Le Rire*, it is also the source of man's feebleness and bathos. Not for nothing did the chains of the magical inference in Frazer's discourse remind Sigmund Freud of the obsessions of the neurotic, which themselves seem to underlie application to difficult tasks, including those of writing *The Golden Bough* or Freud's own *The Psychopathology of Everyday Life*. Madmen under the illusion that they are all-powerful, thinkers convinced that they can change the world, are in this respect very like shamans. That they are so is a modern insight, but one that harks back to the Enlightenment with its protective passion for order and sanity. Indeed, one of the most vivid proleptic illustrations of the disturbances described by Freud—and their affinity with the occult—occurs towards the end of the novella *Rasselas* by that eighteenth century neurotic, lexicographer and polymath, Dr Samuel Johnson. The passage concerns an astronomer convinced that he can control the stars.

Bergson and Freud represent a later stage of modernism to Frazer's, yet like him both of these twentieth-century rationalists possess solid Enlightenment antecedents. Perhaps for this reason, Frazer appears to foreshadow their conclusions, and his humour to draw on related nuances. It is no accident that so many of the social inhibitions mentioned in *Taboo and the Perils of the Soul*, Part Two of *The Golden Bough*, read to us like phobias, with all of the potential for vaudeville such psychological afflictions possess. In expounding them Frazer exercises to the full his talent for burlesque. In New Guinea, we read, in-laws are strictly tabooed: 'Families thus connected by the betrothal of two of their members are not only forbidden to pronounce each other's names; they may not even look at each other, and the rule gives rise to the most comic scenes when they happen to meet accidentally.' Indeed, 'among the natives who inhabit the coast of the Gazelle peninsular in New Britain to mention the name of your brother-in-law is the grossest affront you can offer to him; it is a crime punishable by death'. Names of the deceased are, as Frazer observes, likewise proscribed in many places. In Australia a missionary named Oldfield was unwise enough to shout out the name of a recently dead aboriginal to one of the unfortunate's relatives: 'the man fairly took to his heels and did not venture to show himself again for several days.'

Such instances reveal the existential anxiety, the disorganization of the sensibility behind the efficient and customary front. Nor is his humour blunted when, detailing taboos frequently attached to the names for common things during hunting expeditions, Frazer proceeds to draw most of his examples from the Isle of Lewis.

Frazer brings off effects like this time after time. It his way of suggesting the pervasiveness and brittleness of steadying conventions based on reassuring irrationality. Indeed, much of the effect of his style depends on this reflex, reinforced as it is by a use of the tense that I have called elsewhere the anthropological present. Societies change with time; indeed it is essential to Frazer's message to insist that they do so. To be true to this insight would demand that events and processes are evoked in a range of past tenses, yet when Frazer comes to non-metropolitan societies (which includes that of the Highlanders), he portrays them as trapped in a state of repetitive suspension. The effect is to give the impression that such cultures are burdened by obligations based on beliefs that they dare not, or cannot, renounce. At the same time it is these habits of mind and body that make such people what they are, in all of their attractive—if occasionally sinister—distinctiveness. We moreover—the assumed metropolitan readership—owe much to our ancestors who thought and acted in like fashion: *cum excusatione itqque veteres audiendi sunt* [with just such a plea are the elders meet-to-be-heard]. In this respect Frazer was typical of his age: connoisseur of the exotic, he believed in improvement; paternalist, he valued the strange. This double perspective on systems and peoples required a flexibility of tone and style he plentifully provides. The nineteenth century *fin-de-siècle* was not short of comparative ethnographers, and many of them wrote well. Frazer's eminence lies in his negotiation between interpretative moments: the way in which, in chapter after chapter, volume after engaging volume, he slips from grandiose evolutionary generalisation to empathetically rendered instance, his imagination and his categorising intellect perpetually juxtaposed.

In volume one of *Adonis, Attis Osiris: Studies in the History of Oriental Religion*, Frazer describes the Feast of the Great Goddess Cybele annually celebrated in Asia the city of Hierapolis in the spring. Its climax was a Rite of Blood at which the priests of Attis, eunuchs to a person, cut themselves with blades:

> While the flutes played, the drums beat, and the eunuch priests slashed themselves with knives, the religious excitement gradually spread like a

wave among the crowd of onlookers, and many a one did that which he little thought to do when he came as a holiday spectator to the festival. For man after man, his veins throbbing with music, his eyes fascinated by the sight of streaming blood, flung his garments from him, leaping forth with a shout, and seizing one of the swords which stood ready for purpose, castrated himself on the spot. Then he ran through the city, holding the bloody pieces in his hand, till he threw them into one of the houses which he passed in his mad career. The household thus honoured had to furnish him with a suit of female attire and female ornaments, which he wore for the rest of his life.

The comic finesse of this passage is the product, partly of timing, partly of minor verbal adjustments: the double-entendre on 'holiday', the plural in 'bloody pieces', the adjectival nudge in 'honoured' insinuating the expression of the householder as a set of freshly severed male genitalia comes flying over his wall, the tilt of this particular 'mad career'. No Victorian anthropologist ever steered closer to tragedy, or indeed to farce. More dreadful is the following sentence where, drawing on a celebrated poem by Catullus, Frazer describes the mental condition of the priestly neophyte at the moment his lucidity is restored.

No writer of the Enlightenment, Scottish or otherwise, more effectively demonstrated the effect of 'enthusiasm' on the credulous body and mind. And yet in his *Inquiry* Hume had told of a certain crippled doorkeeper in the cathedral at Saragossa: 'He had been seen for so long a time wanting a leg, but recovered that limb by the rubbing of holy oil upon the stump; and the Cardinal assures us that he saw him with two legs.' Hume styles this a 'singular' miracle. By such slight inflections, the loss of a limb or the gaining, the enlightened and the modern intellect chastises national faith.

A Retrospective View of
James Leslie Mitchell

William K. Malcolm

On the ice-clear forenoon of 13 February, 2001 I found myself slithering through the slushy dubs covering the farm track bumping down to the abandoned croft of Hillhead of Seggat, nestling in the rolling farmland at Auchterless near Turriff. En route to the inaugural celebration of the centenary of James Leslie Mitchell's birth being staged at Arbuthnott further south in the Mearns, I stopped off on a lone pilgrimage to the compact wee croft that had heralded Mitchell's arrival in the world. As I picked my way through the sharn in the deserted farmyard and breathed in the chill air of the low Aberdeenshire hills, I ruminated upon the bracing simplicity of a setting which had helped to forge the creative sensibility of a writer who has been steadily appreciated and applauded throughout the world. Tentative plans to preserve 'Hillies' for its literary associations have not yet borne fruit. Yet it was perfectly apt that the passage of time should be so sharply delineated by the present derelication of croft and byre, providing an emblem of the principle of universal change which was such a poignant keynote in *Sunset Song* and which became Lewis Grassic Gibbon's abiding philosophical refrain in his epic trilogy *A Scots Quair*.

The centenary of a writer's birth provides fresh impetus—at a suitably detached remove—for critical rediscovery, for objective reappraisal and for holistic revaluation. The centenary of the birth of James Leslie Mitchell, popularised via the sobriquet of Lewis Grassic Gibbon, is more timely than most, given his cruelly abbreviated lifespan. His early death, at not yet thirty four, away back in February 1935 allows us now to form comfortable judgements regarding his final achievement, based upon informed insight that has built up in the intervening decades. Typecast for many years as a social chronicler who charted the tragedy of rural decline in northeast Scotland, Leslie Mitchell is now apprehended as a much more versatile, ambitious and original artist, both in Scotland and beyond.

While the groundbreaking biography from 1966, *Leslie Mitchell: Lewis Grassic Gibbon* (1) collated the principle facts of Leslie Mitchell's life, drawing upon evidence of family, friends and acquaintances as well as personal papers and manuscripts, it was littered with errors. Unfortunately Ian S Munro died before he could fulfil his intention to produce a revised and emended version. However, Ian Munro himself would have conceded that his book was not a critical analysis of Mitchell's writing, leaning too heavily on a trawl of Mitchell's press agency cuttings albums. The equally damaging complaint may be levelled at Munro that his portrait has been airbrushed to sanitise his subject's political mettle and radical literary aims.

Since Munro's biography, particular elements in Leslie Mitchell's life story have assumed new importance. Firstly, the source of his genius seems even more startling and elusive now, to those in full possession of the mundane facts of his background and education. The enigma ascribed by Gibbon himself to the origins of Mungo Park's father in Niger may in fact be applied with even greater facility to his own roots: 'Where he came from there is no knowing, except from the soil, up out of its darkness with that horde of men of like kind, the dour even-tempered peasants of Scotland'. (2) Yet Leslie Mitchell's spectacular intellectual and academic development, and his absurd gifts with language, evolving in almost complete isolation, set him apart from his peers. Formal records show that he was almost completely alone within his family, where both mother and father, stemming from well established north-east rural working class backgrounds, were baffled by the literary prodigy born in their midst. In addition, his fellow siblings George and John, both born to a different father, were distanced from their younger half-brother by blood as well as by temperament and ability. The role of Alexander Gray, Mitchell's second dominie at Arbuthnott School, thus appears even more vital to young Leslie's development. A mercurial and intense pupil, Leslie Mitchell required skilful handling in an age when individuality and forthrightness were not highly prized in Scottish education, and when the traditional Kailyard stereotype of the nobly achieving 'lad o' pairts' proved largely mythical. Alexander Gray, as a young graduate with enlightened ideas and, even more crucially, with almost identical farming roots at nearby Dunnottar, became Mitchell's mentor and ally—and in later years, despite the fifteen year age difference, his close friend (although, with touching formality, Mitchell studiously addressed his former teacher as 'Mr Gray' throughout their lives). The positive influence of Alexander Gray is even more prominent when compared with Mitchell's subsequent school career at Mackie Academy in Stonehaven, where his precociousness promoted friction with authority which smouldered steadily before culminating in a final explosion earning him formal expulsion from his final source of full-time education, aged sixteen. School records from this time lapsed during the war, but local anecdotage testifying to a final confrontation over politics between Mitchell and one of the more authoritarian teachers rings true.

Mitchell's subsequent struggle to earn a living in journalism—first in Aberdeen with *The Aberdeen Journal* and thereafter in Glasgow with *The Scottish Farmer*—has been well documented. (3) More revealing in hindsight, however, is the radical political blooding that this phase in Mitchell's life embodied. Young Leslie's social sympathies were already fully elicited by his participation in his own family's commitment to the unremitting treadmill of subsistence farming on the Mearns croft of Bloomfield high up on the Reisk, a holding that was notoriously poor, being small, exposed to the elements and poorly drained. In Aberdeen, Mitchell's political education began in earnest, famously coming to a head in the fiery platform address that he delivered during the foundation of the Aberdeen Soviet launched in the wake of the Russian Revolution in 1917. Mitchell's move to Glasgow coincided exactly with the dramatic protests mounted in George Square on 'Bloody Friday' on 31 January, 1919, and as his mature essay on 'Glasgow' in *Scottish Scene* amply demonstrates, his six month experience of 'Red Clydeside' thirled him to a lifetime of political activism campaigning for the welfare of the ordinary people. His dismissal from the *Farmer*—covertly recreated in his second novel, *The Thirteenth Disciple* (4)— spelt personal and family shame and professional disaster. Yet the political motivation behind Mitchell's fumbling attempt to fiddle his journalistic expenses marks a formative step in the establishment of the personal priorities of the writer who cast himself firmly in his mature writing as a 'revolutionist'. (5)

Emotional collapse followed this trauma, which effectively marked the termination of Mitchell's journalistic aspirations. The desperation behind Mitchell's last gasp effort at survival, his enlistment in the RASC in 1919, is therefore tangible. Mitchell was totally unsuited to the mindless routines of army life, to the demands to conform to rigid codes and rules and set modes of thought and behaviour. He was also temperamentally and ideologically at odds with the violent means and ends underpinning military service. Yet his three and a half years of exotic travel in Mesopotamia, Central Asia, Persia and Egypt stimulated his imagination, providing the raw material for later fiction such as *The Calends of Cairo, Persian Dawns, Egyptian Nights* and *The Lost Trumpet*, and hugely expanding his picture of the world.

Mitchell's 'lost' six months following his army discharge in 1923 were reclaimed dramatically in 1989 when Mary Thomson, an Australian emigrée, published a first hand account of her encounter with Leslie Mitchell while she was fostered with the Mitchells at Bloomfield—a not unusual social exigency at that time in the northeast of Scotland. Mrs Thomson's memoir affords fleeting insight to the depths of Mitchell's despair at this juncture, portraying a lonely and troubled soul retrieving some measure of comfort from visits to familiar childhood haunts while passing the life of a recluse within the strained atmosphere of the family home. (6)

Escape to the Forces again in the early Twenties emerged as the only viable alternative to this strange limbo in his life; the extensive period of six years for which Mitchell committed himself to the RAF betrays increased anxiety and a profound sense of insecurity regarding his future prospects. The RAF stint, stationed as a clerk at various posts in the south of England, involved much more mundane duties than his RASC service had done but bestowed no greater sense of purpose. Leslie Mitchell coasted in a day job that was undemanding but which provided his bread and butter on a reliable basis. His personal life in this period was contrastingly eventful, however. He experienced the thrill of the newspaper publication of his first story, 'Siva Plays the Game', in 1924; he secured personal stability with his marriage in 1925 to Rebecca Middleton, a former neighbour at Arbuthnott whom he had courted, miraculously, throughout his distant army travels; removal to the bustle of London in Shepherd's Bush in December, 1927 took him to the cultural heart of Britain, with invaluable resources such as the British Museum to hand; *Hanno*, his first book, a speculative essay on the future of exploration, appeared in June, 1928; and he earned the satisfaction of winning a regular short story slot in the well respected literary magazine, Leonard Huxley's *The*

Cornhill. Typically, Mitchell also participated in semi-serious political subversion in the south of England at this time, producing with his friend Stuart Parham an in-house newspaper of challengingly disreputable character called *The Kenley Kronikle.*

The most telling experience from this phase in Leslie Mitchell's life was more painful, however, as is vividly borne out by unique family letters from 1926 held in the National Library of Scotland, formally released for public perusal only last year. (7) This folio of correspondence between Leslie and Ray Mitchell traces in excoriating detail the trauma of Ray's miscarriage and the death of the young couple's first child. Leslie Mitchell's letters provide moving testimony to his emotional and spiritual coruscation by the trauma, as he gradually finds consolation from the loss in the convalescence of his wife. This personal tragedy sustained the recurring motif in Mitchell's writings of images capturing the dangers and hardships of childbirth—a motif which develops in Leslie Mitchell's hands into a shocking and challenging feminist statement. (8)

The remaining five and a half adrenaline-fuelled years in which Leslie Mitchell finally pursued his vocation as a self-styled 'professional writer-cratur' (9) bear witness to astonishing reserves of intellectual energy and imaginative fecundity. The visible tip of the iceberg takes the form of sixteen further full length volumes of a staggering range and diversity (but all of residual quality), supplemented by a wealth of occasional publications encompassing stories, essays, book reviews and journalism. Yet Mitchell's papers acquired by the National Library of Scotland in 1981 tell an even more spectacular tale of manuscripts repeatedly rejected and revised, of new work endlessly in progress, of failed experiments in drama and poetry, of mothballed plans and a host of tantalising new projects including gargantuan histories of mankind and of religion, a uniform series of books on the ancient past, a Scottish *Spartacus* about William Wallace, a trilogy of novels set in Scottish Covenanting times and an autobiography. However, the practical reality of Mitchell's professional darg is quite grim, as his meticulously arranged file of publishers' contracts starkly chronicles an author's unavailing struggle to earn a passable living by wheedling miniscule improvements in advances on royalties and on percentage terms.

Mitchell's life story is thus the very stuff of one of his own melodramas, with his hard-won artistic achievement standing at odds with the unpropitious circumstances from which it was wrenched. As if his personal history was not sufficiently dramatic, it also transpires that Mitchell indulged from time to time in playful embellishment of the biographical facts. He conjured up a wholly apocryphal past as an archaeologist in Yucatan for a reporter on *The Glasgow Evening News*; he took liberties with his educational background for an American publisher for whom he fabricated attendance at 'Scottish private universities' on the blurb of *The Lost Trumpet*; and he even concocted the gloriously bizarre physical recreation of 'deep-sea diving' for his entry in *Who's Who*. (10) A witty and gregarious socialite, Leslie Mitchell's impish sense of humour constantly spilled over into his writing even to the extent of deliberately distorting his own life history.

The passage of over six decades since the jarring shock of his death from peritonitis has provided firm ground for appreciation of the personal values which motivated Leslie Mitchell as a man and as a writer. A writer who can best be classified as an exponent of French Marxist Louis Aragon's definition of '*littérature engagée*', (11) Mitchell was consumed by a passionate interest in human rights in all spheres. Very much a political animal, his left wing political beliefs remained deeply entrenched from his youth, although inevitably the outlet that they received in terms of party affiliation—particularly in Glasgow—at times remains obscure. However, while he indulged the imaginative writer's prerogative to strike maverick political poses, Leslie Mitchell's political radicalism is never less than genuinely felt and passionately expressed; the rogue quality is largely attributable to the urgency of his search for social and political solutions, as opposed to the cavalier and downright contrary posturing of his friend Hugh MacDiarmid.

The basic pattern of Leslie Mitchell's political development after he was plunged into the world of revolutionary politics towards the end of the First World War is one of steadily maintained ardency and militancy. His fiction and non-fiction possess a trenchant moral charge which constantly sought an outlet in the pursuit of radical political solutions to the pressing social problems of the inter-war years. Driven by such a powerful moral force, Mitchell's politics subsequently oscillated between an idealistic anarchism and a hard-line communism. Diffusionism—the arcane historical view of human evolution as constituting a freakish decline from primitive purity to civilised depravity—provided Mitchell with a convenient means of salvaging belief in man's essential goodness, at a time when he was all too aware of the decline in moral, social, political, spiritual values in the wasteland years attending the First World War. Mitchell concisely summarised his colourful political development in the course of a chatty letter to Naomi Mitchison in 1933, outlining what he termed the intimate 'history of a revoluter':

I suppose I'm still some kind of revolutionary. I was thrown out of the Communist Party as a Trotskyist—while I was in the ranks of the Army, doing Communist propaganda. So I went Anarchist for a bit, but they're such damn fools, with their blah about Kropotkin (whose anthropology is worse than Frazer's) and Bakunin. When the last Labour Gov went west, I re-applied to join the Communists, but they refused to have anything to do with me. Brief history of a revoluter. I once tried (and wrote a propaganda novel for it) to form a Society of Militant Pacifists—chaps who were to engage in sabotage, train-wrecking, and so on if another war came. But the Promethean Society pinched my members. (12)

The reference to Mitchell's blacklisted Trotskyism is most likely apocryphal, given the later appearance of the Trotskyist element in British politics, (13) but there is no doubt that latterly Mitchell was influenced by the Trotskyist tendency among the radical left, particularly with regard to the pursuit of increased strategic flexibility through internal democracy and through increased pluralism in the aftermath of revolution. Perhaps the most accurate representation of Mitchell's mature political stance, however, is the one which characterises him as a 'hidden member' of the CPGB, a sympathiser for whom open declaration of official membership could have proved professionally harmful. Certainly Mitchell's letters to Eric Linklater and his incisive contribution to the British Section of the influential anti-fascist movement Writers International via the seminal journal *Left Review* towards the end of his life confirm that *Grey Granite*'s severe political temper, exemplified by young Ewan Tavendale's political hardening throughout the book, is in quintessence the author's own standpoint. 'I am a revolutionary writer', declared Grassic Gibbon unequivocally in *Left Review*, (14) and in private correspondence with Linklater, he teased out the personal ramifications of this tag:

Thanks for all the nice thinks [sic] about *Grey Granite*, plus your opinions on Communism. Everyone insists on regarding me as a Communist—except the Communist Party of Great Britain, which twice in 1931 refused my application to join. This no doubt showed its good sense. I loathe organization, control, the state, and the voice of the sergeant-major. As the sole surviving specimen of Natural Man to be found in these islands, I'm naturally an anarchist. But how you or I or—more to the point—our unfortunate progeny can attain real freedom and fun without the preliminary conditioning of communism is beyond me. Communism's merely a means to an end—a nannie enforcing on the dirty little boy who calls himself Man the necessity for scrubbing the back of his neck and keeping his regrettable bowels in order. When he grows adolescent and can do these things automatically and has ceased to smell quite so badly, he'll be a much better equipped specimen for his chosen mission of playing football with the cosmos. (15)

Readers' polls conducted in the last two years by James Thin Booksellers and the *Herald* attest that Lewis Grassic Gibbon enjoys a democratic appeal that is absolutely unique in Scotland beyond any writer bar Burns. Yet this popularity within Scotland has actually inhibited a genuine understanding of Mitchell's achievement, causing critical confusion regarding the cultural context that he inhabited, and within which his work now needs to be analysed. While Mitchell himself enjoyed the celebrity that his Scottish 'cousin' Lewis Grassic Gibbon won for him, the invention of a Scottish persona was initially little more than a publicity stunt devised opportunistically to give him licence to double his publishing output without visibly saturating the market. Mitchell himself described the invention of Lewis Grassic Gibbon—derived from his maternal grandmother's name—as a creative convenience in his interview with Louis Katin published in Glasgow's *Evening News* in 1933:

Mitchell is primarily an archaeologist and a Diffusionist. He's not 'national'. But *Sunset Song*, as a realism-romance of Scotland, needed another personality and a different style of writing to bud it forth. Hence Gibbon— which, by the way, is a family name. (16)

In most minds, however, Mitchell morphed into Gibbon, and as a result the runaway success of the Grassic Gibbon writings has unjustly overshadowed Leslie Mitchell's other achievements. Early critics, led inevitably by Mitchell's scurrilously unreliable crony Hugh MacDiarmid, habitually bracketed him with the Scottish Literary Renaissance of the Thirties, hailing his achievement in mainly Nationalist terms. This trend reached its zenith in a particularly misguided article by David Macaree in 1964, unfortunately echoed by J T Low within the critical apparatus for the schools' edition of *Sunset Song* published by Longman in 1971, which foisted an elliptical allegorical meaning upon the trilogy, and upon Sunset Song in particular. (17) Yet despite similar efforts in recent years by Maurice Lindsay, Francis Russell Hart, Douglas Gifford and others, Lewis Grassic Gibbon rests uneasily with the movement collectively referred to as the Scottish Literary Renaissance. (18) Grassic Gibbon came in contact with the leading lights of the Scottish literary scene in the Thirties, from MacDiarmid to the Muirs, Neil Gunn, James Barke and Helen Cruickshank. His work editing *The Voice of Scotland* series of Scottish monographs for Routledge, as the surviving correspondence file testifies, dramatically expanded his Scottish literary contacts among the Scottish diaspora around London and back in Scotland itself. Nevertheless, he himself presented his Scottishness as signifying a cultural interest totally circumscribed by his left-wing scruples and held permanently in check by a deep-seated hatred of fascism. Mitchell expressed his views most coherently in a newspaper article in 1933 when he called himself 'non-Nationalist, and yet interested in this new revival of cultural and political Nationalism'. (19)

A more sympathetic critical perspective has gradually been brought to bear over the years by commentators who have won free of the shackles imposed earlier by MacDiarmid and Macaree. Thanks to erudite critical surveys by Jack Lindsay, David Smith, Andy Croft and Valentine Cunningham, (20) Mitchell has steadily found a place at the heart of the British revolutionary tradition. It has even come to the point now where Mitchell's achievement is automatically expected to feature in any analysis of left-wing British writing. (21) Furthermore, continental critics are increasingly embracing Mitchell as a writer of European stature and importance. Gustav Klaus has spearheaded the rehabilitation proper of Mitchell's reputation, boldly proclaiming *A Scots Quair* in 1978 'the outstanding Socialist prose work of the inter-war period'. (22)

Mitchell does indeed appear unique among the writers of the Thirties. Many proletarian novels from this period appear sadly time-locked. As George Orwell observed, 'orthodox' authors of left wing conviction can be supremely well-intentioned but artistically unenterprising (23) —Walter Brierley, Harold Heslop, Lewis Jones and Walter Greenwood, earnest working class champions all, slide into this category. Conversely, the work of more notable stylists like

John Cornford, Naomi Mitchison and the Auden group tend to be devalued by inescapable marks of the authors' fundamental disenfranchisement from the working classes themselves. Leslie Mitchell alone combined audacious literary skills with a committed left wing sensibility honed upon authentic first hand knowledge of working class experience. Chris Guthrie's peasant smeddum may lack political direction, but it is not in any way lacking in moral and emotional engagement at a grass roots level. In fact, the dynamic tension existing between her political despair and young Ewan's idealism is the fundamental dichotomy animating Leslie Mitchell's mature left wing outlook.

The primary achievement of Lewis Grassic Gibbon is essentially stylistic, as his flexible prose hybrid opened up dramatically Mitchell's capacity for self-expression. Neologistic experimentation marries with surely quarried colloquial idioms in a compelling narrative which lurches from ribald humour to tender lyricism to gut-wrenching pathos. Yet the wealth of ideology underpinning Mitchell's English writings is absolutely identical in nature, fudging the distinction between JLM and LGG. Among his 'English' work, however, only in *Spartacus* does Mitchell fully emulate the creative achievement of *A Scots Quair*.

Contrived cameos of Leslie Mitchell's artistic schizophrenia, drawing upon MacDiarmid's appropriation of Gregory Smith's vision of the dynamic contrariness of the Scottish creative instinct dubbed 'The Caledonian Antisyzygy', appear increasingly wide of the mark. (24) In particular, the notion of Mitchell preserving a completely separate typewriter for Grassic Gibbon's literary efforts is exploded by appreciation of the sheer unrelenting volume and multiplicity of his literary endeavours in his last years. Viewed as a totality, his personal ideology and his literary corpus possess a convincing consistency and coherence.

Leslie Mitchell's literary reputation has grown steadily over the decades since his death, although the LGG works have unfairly eclipsed his others. Of course, the shock waves endure following Grassic Gibbon's explosion upon the Scottish literary scene in August 1932 to widespread acclaim, in Scotland and England and, quickly afterwards, in America, with the idiomatic and narrative spontaneity of *Sunset Song* finding an enthusiastic response in all walks of life. Almost inevitably, his native Northeast was characteristically thrawn in its reception of the book, with Aberdeen City Libraries epitomising local prudishness by banning the novel from public borrowing. And Gibbon even launched into an impassioned attack in print in reply to one not untypically ignorant review in *The Fife Herald and Journal* which, among a litany of misguided complaints, questioned the accuracy of the book's 'description of crofter girls' under-clothing of that period', asserted that 'the coarse bits of the book are in italic type' and concluded that the novel was 'crude' and 'no credit to Scotland'. (25) Of course, sensitive observers like Neil Gunn, Compton MacKenzie and MacDiarmid hailed first *Sunset Song* and subsequently the whole trilogy as a landmark in Scottish literature. James Barke's unbridled admiration for Gibbon's achievement is quite infectious and spontaneous, as he wrote immediately to the author:

Well Gibbon man I read *Sunset Song* with greater and richer and fuller and deeper enjoyment than anything I can ever remember reading. With the possible exception of *The Communist Manifesto*—on a different plane. (26)

Mitchell archly consolidated his position at the vanguard of Scottish writing with *Cloud Howe* and *Grey Granite*, finely crafted sequels to his first novel, with the irrepressible miscellany *Scottish Scene*—a book conceived and shaped by him, despite the joint crediting accorded to Hugh MacDiarmid—with *Niger*, his provocative portrait of Mungo Park, and with a series of occasional letters, stories, articles and book reviews posted in Scottish cultural papers like *The Free Man*. The Mitchell writings, from his adventure romances and his science fiction to his exotic short stories and his historical and biographical reconstructions, are never less than vividly alive, yet they have struggled consistently to maintain critical parity with those of Gibbon. Even the sweeping historical novel *Spartacus*, which represents the most perfect embodiment of Leslie Mitchell's political ideals, had to wait until 1970 for a short-lived republication by Hutchinson.

Letters to various publishers from Mitchell's last years pestering them for new commissions suggest that he was in danger of over-playing the commercial potential of Lewis Grassic Gibbon. Extant plans for his autobiography, for his William Wallace novel, for his Covenanters' trilogy and for a new Scottish novel set around Stonehaven were met warily by publishers' readers. And at his death, following the traditional flurry of panegyrics from all sides, his memory was kept alive by a select band of loyal followers led by Ray Mitchell and including MacDiarmid and Ivor Brown.

Plans for a commemorative *festschrift* unfortunately foundered only a few years after Mitchell died. (27) And even the Quair was allowed to slip quietly from the shelves towards the end of the war.

From this sad nadir, modest signs of a revival emerged with the release of the first single-volume edition of the trilogy in 1946. But interest in Mitchell only really revived with Ian Munro's biography twenty years later, followed the next year by Munro's popular miscellany of Gibbon's *Scottish Scene* writings bulked out with selected English stories and school essays, *A Scots Hairst*. This precipitated a welcome upsurge in LGG's fortunes. After the one-off reappearance of *Spartacus* in 1970, the fondly remembered BBC television dramatisation of *Sunset Song* directed by Pharic MacLaren simultaneously helped to claim a niche for J T Lowe's educational edition of the novel for Longman in the Higher English syllabus of many Scottish secondary schools from 1971. Students hooked by the rural novel could then pursue the remainder of the trilogy in the pulp paperbacks released by Pan in 1973. This successful entry to Scottish secondary schools can be seen in hindsight as the watershed in Leslie Mitchell's rediscovery, providing the bedrock for future study and for increased critical understanding.

Even so, publishers have been disappointingly slow to catch the wave of popular interest that has accrued from the early nineteen seventies. *Scottish Scene* made a small-scale reappearance in 1974, thanks to Portway's reprint at the behest of the London Library Association. Mitchell's intriguing second novel *The Thirteenth Disciple* enjoyed a brief revival as part of Paul Harris's percipient Scottish Fiction Reprint Library in 1981. *The Speak of the Mearns*, an unfinished novella in Gibbon's unmistakable idiom, belatedly became publicly available in 1982. *Three Go Back* made a somewhat apologetic return to the bookshelves as part of Greenhill's obscure science fiction series in 1986. And *Spartacus* at long last appeared in a worthy critical edition as part of The Association for Scottish Literary Studies' Scottish Classics series in 1990. Most important of all, Tom Crawford's scrupulous scholarship provided definitive annotated texts of *A Scots Quair* for Canongate's Scottish Classics from 1988 to 1990. The boom in Scottish publishing (and republication) in recent years has had a healthy spin-off, with B&W reviving *The Thirteenth Disciple* and *Spartacus* in recent years and Polygon embarking last year upon a rolling programme of complete republication of Leslie Mitchell's major works (including the miscellany gathered under the title *The Speak of the Mearns*) in a uniform format. This year, even Mitchell's synopses and poetry have found publication in Canongate's mighty rag-bag, *Smeddum*.

Readers abroad also are increasingly well served, with Schocken Books of New York keeping the trilogy popularly available across the Atlantic, and with translations having appeared in Germany, France and Japan. And although Mitchell's surviving correspondence runs to just over two hundred items, unique caches discovered recently, including letters to James Barke, Eric Linklater, Naomi Mitchison, Dorothy Tweed and Tom Wintringham as well as to publishers like George Routledge, augment the surviving hoard held in public hands to yield significant biographical and critical insights. Collectively, these informal writings take us as close as we can now come to the author's everyday voice; it is to be hoped that the centenary may finally make possible publication of such fascinating subsidiary material as extant correspondence and literary notebooks. Ray Mitchell, who died in 1978 following a lifetime staunchly promoting her husband's writing, would have been truly thankful for this long-overdue attention. There is indeed something almost dream-like about the recent spate of reprints for those ardent enthusiasts formerly doomed to years of fruitless rummaging in second-hand bookshops for priceless J Leslie Mitchell first editions.

Mitchell's writing has generated minor criticism of gloriously diverse character and substance from his own lifetime onwards, as well as a handful of full-length studies that have appeared periodically in the last thirty years. His most enduring works have sustained, to varying degrees of rigour and penetration, Marxist, Nationalist, feminist and, most recently, Post-colonialist interpretations. (28) While Mitchell deserves a modern biography balancing informed research with sympathetic insight, full-length studies, following Ian Munro's original life history, have proved arresting in their diversity. Douglas Young's *Beyond the Sunset* offered a pioneering critical overview measured against his consuming interest in Diffusionism; Douglas Gifford has produced an invigorating comparison with Neil Gunn; Ian Campbell covers his life and works with verve and economy; the present author's monograph from the same time sets the primary and secondary works within an appropriate ideological framework; Peter Whitfield has mined some fresh biographical and historical details; Clarke Geddes has created an unusual fictionalised account of his life; and most recently, Uwe Zagratzki has made a measured study of Mitchell's utopian politics in his writings. (29) Yet, like all truly great imaginative writers, ultimately Leslie Mitchell defies classification.

Leslie Mitchell's best writings—principally, those published under the name of Grassic Gibbon—have a stylistic vitality that, according to his own letters and essays, he worked hard to attain. He was an omnivorous reader from his schooldays; within a few years of departing Mackie Academy, he was immersing himself in the flowery wordiness of Georgian literature and gleefully devouring by the shelfload weighty historical tomes—in various languages—at the British Museum. As an impressively-read polymath, subsequently Mitchell's his own fictive approach is indebted to technical advances made by continental models such as Anatole France, Ignazio Silone and, most directly of all, by the Soviet socialist realists Gorki and Gladkov. Mitchell even traded on his cosmopolitan tastes by providing introductions for English translations of Heinrich Mann's *The Blue Angel* and Peter Freuchen's *Eskimo*. (30) Yet paradoxically, his best work is a testament to his ability to do the basics supremely well, with vigorous narrative drive being accompanied by sensitive character development and unremitting immediacy of expression. Thematically, his major achievements are predicated upon the simple, wholesome values summed up in the *Sunset Song* quotation inscribed on his gravestone : 'The kindness of friends and the warmth of toil and the peace of rest'. Accordingly, the elemental purity of *Sunset Song*'s fresh sensory impressions of 'the sweetness of the Scottish land and skies' places Mitchell comfortably in the international tradition of classics of rural realism such as Zola's *The Earth*, Hamsun's *Growth of The Soil*, Laxness's *Independent People*, Silone's *Fontamara*, Sholokhov's *Tikhi Don* and Steinbeck's *The Grapes of Wrath*. Yet even this classification denigrates what Mitchell finally accomplished in his best work.

Sympathetic understanding of LGG's own view of his trilogy as a single uniform whole has gradually undermined the earlier misconception of the series as comprising one book-of-a-lifetime followed by a rushed sequel, capped by a concluding volume completely botched due to pressure of work and ill health. (31) Thankfully, *Cloud Howe* and *Grey Granite* individually have since come in from the cold. (32) However, Leslie Mitchell initially conceived the *Quair* as a uniform entity, writing shortly before his death of his aim of seeing a revised, single volume edition through the press. (33) Appreciation of the artistic integrity underlying the whole trilogy identifies LGG's work as something much greater than the sum of its component parts—an epic *tour de force* combining comedy and tragedy, lyricism and melodrama, realism and romance; it is a vivid social commentary, a revolutionary novel, a love story and a sanguine vision of natural epiphany all rolled harmoniously into one. The Marxist critic Jack Lindsay put his finger on the prime reason behind the trilogy's durability, hailing it away back in 1946 as 'the kind of work which keeps on growing with history'. (34) The trilogy remains the most effective and complete artistic synthesis of Leslie Mitchell's moral and social ideals as well as the most perfect expression of his philosophical belief in an infinitely changing universal life force. The book's sure political aesthetic bends to fit the specific temper of the times—providing equally damning correlatives for the reactionary excesses of the Thatcherite government and for New Labour's smoothly groomed self-interest. In addition, the author's contemporary responses are firmly embedded in principles—social, moral, political and philosophical—that are compelling and timeless.

Leslie Mitchell was more aware than most of the precarious nature of celebrity in Scotland, where on the one hand he perceived Burns being uncomprehendingly lionised, while on the other he himself, along with George Blake, suffered from the niggling parochialism manifested in the stock put-down, 'I kent his faither!' (35) With the advent of the centenary of Leslie Mitchell's birth, however, it is safe to state that his literary reputation is now secure. Lewis Grassic Gibbon has been popularised by adaptations on radio, television and stage, (36) while plans are afoot to realise his own ambition to translate *Sunset Song* into a feature film. Centenary events, ranging from conferences to lectures, to drama, to art exhibitions, have been staged in Aberdeen, Edinburgh, Glasgow, Rostock—and, most strikingly, in Arbuthnott. Leslie Mitchell's rehabilitation is symbolised finally by the establishment at Arbuthnott almost ten years ago of The Grassic Gibbon Centre, an independent charity set up by the local folk to promote Mitchell's life and work. While the Centre evolved naturally as an organic part of the social fabric of Mitchell's home area, its swelling contacts emphasise the truly global nature of Leslie Mitchell's appeal: Friends of the Centre can be found in France, Germany, Spain, Italy, Japan, Russia and America, as well as across the length and breadth of the British Isles.

James Leslie Mitchell's early death becomes even more shocking with every year that passes. Yet the sharpness of the loss was assuaged to some extent in the centenary year (2001) by the international recognition that his work is gaining across the world.

Notes

1. Ian S Munro, *Leslie Mitchell: Lewis Grassic Gibbon*, Oliver & Boyd, Edinburgh, 1966.

2. Lewis Grassic Gibbon, *Niger: The Life of Mungo Park*, The Porpoise Press, Edinburgh, p.10.

3. The original typescript of Grassic Gibbon's pithy essay on 'Aberdeen' published in Scottish Scene in 1934 provides the most vibrant account of young Leslie Mitchell's youthful idealism in his first place of employment (National Library of Scotland, NLS MSS26050). The Glasgow years have been well chronicled in his essay on 'Glasgow' in that volume, and in John Manson, 'Grassic Gibbon's Glasgow', in *Scottish Labour History Review*, no.10, Winter 1996/Spring 1997, pp.12-13.

4. James Leslie Mitchell, *The Thirteenth Disciple,* Paul Harris, Edinburgh, pp.108-111.

The reality of Mitchell's experience with *The Scottish Farmer* is clearly outlined by Angus MacDonald in *The Scottish Farmer: One Hundred Years*, Outram Magazines, East Kilbride, 1993, pp.45-47.

5. Mitchell's self-description is from 'Controversy: Writers' International (British Section)', in *Left Review*, 1, no.5, February, 1935, pp.179-80.

6. Mary Thomson, 'My Friend Lewis Grassic Gibbon', in *The Scots Magazine*, 131, no.6, September, 1989, pp.602-607.

7. See Karen McVeigh, 'Tragedy that haunted Grassic Gibbon', in *Scotland on Sunday*, 1 October, 2000, p.9.

The folio in question is available for consultation at The National Library of Scotland, NLS MS26063.

8. Such scenes appear in Mitchell's first two novels, *Stained Radiance* and *The Thirteenth Disciple*, and most memorably in *Sunset Song* and *Cloud Howe*.

9. The tag is from a proud letter from Mitchell to Alexander Gray, dated 29 September, 1929, NLS MS26109.

10. Louis Katin, 'Author of Sunset Song', in *The Evening News*, 16 February, 1933, p.6; J Leslie Mitchell, *The Lost Trumpet*, The Bobbs-Merrill Company, Indianapolis, 1932; *Who Was Who*, 3, Adam & Charles Black, London, 1941, p.947.

11. See Max Adereth, 'What is "Littérature Engagée"?', in David Craig, ed., *Marxists on Literature*, Penguin, Harmondsworth, 1975, pp.445-485.

12. Letter, Mitchell to Naomi Mitchison, dated 10 August,1933, NLS Acc.5885.

13. Reg Groves, in *The Balham Group: How British Trotskyism Began*, Pluto Press, London, 1974, pinpoints the inception of British Trotkyism at May, 1932, several years after Mitchell's imperfect recollection. John Callaghan, in his definitive study, *British Trotskyism: Theory and Pratice*, Basil Blackwell, London, 1984, corroborates this dating.

14. Lewis Grassic Gibbon, 'Controversy: Writers' International (British Section)', in *Left Review*, op.cit.1.

15. Letter, Mitchell to Eric Linklater, dated 10 November, 1934, NLS Acc.10282.

16. Louis Katin, 'Author of Sunset Song', op.cit.

17. David Macaree, 'Myth and Allegory in Lewis Grassic Gibbon's A Scots Quair', in *Studies in Scottish Literature*, 2, part 1, July, 1964, pp.45-55.

18. Maurice Lindsay, *History of Scottish Literature*, Robert Hale, London, 1977, pp.414-16; Francis Russell Hart, *The Scottish Novel: A Critical Survey*, John Murray, London, 1978, pp. 229-41; Douglas Gifford, *Neil M Gunn and Lewis Grassic Gibbon*, Oliver & Boyd, Edinburgh, 1983.

19. Lewis Grassic Gibbon, 'News of Battle : Queries for Mr. Whyte', in *The Free Man*, 3, 17 March, 1934, p.9.

20. Jack Lindsay, *After the Thirties: The Novel in Britain and its Future*, Lawrence & Wishart, London, 1956, p.48-54; David Smith, *Socialist Propaganda in the Twentieth-Century British Novel*, Macmillan, London, 1978, chapter eight on *A Scots Quair*; Valentine Cunningham, *British Writers of the Thirties*, Oxford University Press, Oxford, 1988, *passim*; Andy Croft, *Red Letter Days: British Fiction in the 1930s*, Lawrence and Wishart, London, 1990, pp.173-4, 227-8.

21. For example, *A Scots Quair* fits snugly into Ian Haywood's compact survey, *Working-class Fiction from Chartism to Trainspotting*, Northcote House, Plymouth, 1997.

22. Gustav Klaus, 'Socialist Fiction in the 1930s: Some preliminary observations', in *The 1930s: A Challenge to Orthodoxy*, edited by John Lucas, Harvester, Hassocks, 1978, p.32

23. George Orwell, 'Politics and the English Language', *in Inside the Whale and Other Essays*, Penguin, Harmondsworth, 1960, p.152 (originally published in April, 1946).

24. See Hugh MacDiarmid, 'The Caledonian Antisyzygy and the Gaelic

Idea', in *Selected Essays of Hugh MacDiarmid*, edited by Duncan Glen, Jonathan Cape, London, 1969, pp.56-74; Ian Campbell, *Lewis Grassic Gibbon*, Scottish Academic Press, Edinburgh, 1985.

25.　*The Fife Herald and Journal*, 21 September, 1932, p.2.

26.　James Barke, letter to Gibbon, dated 12 December, 1932, Mitchell Library.

27.　See Ian Campbell, 'A Tribute that Never Was: The Plan for A Lewis Grassic Gibbon *Festschrift*', in *Studies in Scottish Literature*, 20, 1985, pp.219-30.

28.　Jack Mitchell has provided the best Marxist interpretation in 'The Struggle for the Working-Class Novel in Scotland, 1900-39', in *Zeitschrift fur Anglistik und Amerikanistik*, 21, 1973, pp.396-403; the most telling Nationalist exploration is Neil M Gunn's 'Nationalism in Writing: Tradition and Magic in the Work of Lewis Grassic Gibbon', in *The Scots Magazine*, October, 1938, pp.28-35; the most probing feminist study is Deirdre Burton's 'A Feminist Reading of Lewis Grassic Gibbon's A Scots Quair', in *The British Working-Class Novel in the Twentieth Century*, edited by Jeremy Hawthorn, Edward Arnold, London, pp.35-46; and a deftly Post-colonialist assessment has been approached by Carla Sassi, in 'Gibbon, Mitchell and Said', in *The Speak of the Place*, 1, no.4, Spring, 1999, pp.1-3.

29.　Full details of these and other critical works on Mitchell are contained in the regularly updated bibliography on The Grassic Gibbon Centre's website, at http://www.grassicgibbon.com

30.　The most complete bibliography of Leslie Mitchell's published works is contained in William K Malcolm, *A Blasphemer & Reformer: A Study of James Leslie Mitchell/Lewis Grassic Gibbon*, AUP, Aberdeen, 1984, pp.200-202.

31.　Ivor Brown is the instigator-in-chief of this crude viewpoint, writing disingenuously in the Foreword to the single volume edition of the trilogy published in 1946 that, 'the great pattern appears to crumble in the author's hands, and the talent, which had been so finely maturing, suddenly seems younger and cruder'.

32.　See Thomas Crawford's typically invigorating introductions to the respective volumes for Canongate Classics in 1989 and 1990.

33.　Mitchell, letter to Neil M Gunn, dated 19 November, 1934, NLS Dep.209.

34.　Jack Lindsay, 'Lewis Grassic Gibbon: A Great Scots Novelist—The

Cycle of Industrialization', in *Decay and Renewal: Critical Essays on Twentieth Century Writing*, Lawrence & Wishart, London, 1976, p.167.

35. Lewis Grassic Gibbon, 'Canting Humbug!', in *The Mearns Leader*, 8 February, 1934, p.1; Lewis Grassic Gibbon, 'I Kent his Faither!', in *Glasgow Evening News* (Saturday Supplement), 24 February, 1934, p.1.

36. Full details of the popular radio and television adaptations of LGG's work are given in William K Malcolm, 'James Leslie Mitchell/Lewis Grassic Gibbon Checklist: Additions III', in *The Bibliotheck*, 11, no.6, 1983, pp.149-156.

Nairn, Nation and Nationalism

Ronald Turnbull

Neal Ascherson has recently described Tom Nairn as 'the dominant political philosopher of his country'. Certainly, in any adequate history of cultural and political debate in Scotland in the last quarter of the twentieth century Nairn will have to be accorded a prominent place.

Nairn is almost a unique figure on the Scottish cultural scene in that he has developed a theory of modern Scottish historical development—'theory' in the sense of a comprehensive *explanatory* account, which refers to economics, politics, culture and psychology, and seeks to establish how these domains are connected. The project is exceptional in a number of ways. In its scope and ambition, it goes well beyond normal exercises in academic historiography. Its political seriousness and refusal of (putative) value-freedom are an affront to academic culture in general. These are some of the reasons why his work has largely been disregarded by professional historians. The theory has also deeply shaped cultural-political discussion in Scotland over the past thirty years or so, not only because it has attracted support, but also, and perhaps more importantly, because it has provoked criticism in the form of reactions which in turn have served to establish new frameworks of debate.

At the same time, and at least since his days as a member—along with Ascherson and other prominent figures—of the Edinburgh branch of the socialist-and-nationalist Scottish Labour Party which was set up by Jim Sillars in December, 1975, Nairn has been a consistent supporter of the Scottish nationalist cause, though he is a nationalist with a small 'n': he has often been highly critical of the ethos and of the strategies of the Scottish National Party. However, over the years there has been a radical change—which, as far as I know, is not explicitly acknowledged in Nairn's published work—in the kind of reasons he provides in justification of this political stance.

This paper is a critical discussion of aspects of Nairn's theory of Scottish history and culture, his arguments for Scottish independence, his theory of nationalism, and of some of the ways in which these interrelate.

1.

Nationalism—or the doctrine that to each culture or nation there ought to correspond a state—is, Nairn takes it, the dominant political principle of modernity. In Europe—to look no further—in the nineteenth and early twentieth centuries, and then again after the disintegration of Soviet socialism, allegiance to this principle fuelled movements for unification (Germany, Italy), or, the more usual case, secession (Greece, Poland, Catholic Ireland, Finland, Norway; Latvia, Slovakia, Slovenia, etc.). Nairn's theorisation of modern Scottish history starts from the fact that, in the classic age of European nationalism—1800-1920—, there was no Scottish nationalist movement worthy of the name. Scotland had, so to speak, turned its back on the dominant modern political principle.

Essentially, Nairn argues (in The *Break-Up of Britain* (1977)) that Scotland's incorporation into and prolonged acquiescence in membership of the British state, and thus its failure to follow the 'normal' trajectory of nations towards development and democracy, have had devastating cultural and psychological consequences. In 'normal' modern conditions, peripheries progress by embracing nationalism, of which the cultural correlate is romanticism. In Scotland, the bourgeoisie and institutional elites opted for a non-nationalist route of remunerative impuissance and servility. There was thus no political requirement for a Scottish romantic movement, and there was no such movement. Instead, according to Nairn, in the nineteenth century Scottish high culture—at least beyond the spheres of science and technology—simply disintegrated. And popular culture, unleavened by any high cultural movement, became singularly mindless and kitsch-ridden. The whole of recent Scottish cultural history, Nairn in fact comes close to saying, can be exhaustively described by reference to the sentimental escapism which many critics have seen as the hallmark of the kailyard school of literature, and to celebration of a fake, show, 'highlandist' identity. At the same time, the choice of the non-nationalist route, of the aspiration at most to manage, but not rule, made cringing subservience the dominant national psychological trait.

This very bald statement gives little indication of the ferocity of Nairn's account, in which words such as 'freakish', 'lunatic', 'deformed' and 'pathological' are liberally applied to describe modern Scottish cultural and psychological conditions.

Of course about this we need to historicise, by taking into account the nature of the standard historical treatments of Scotland on which Nairn's analysis partly relied. He was writing at a time when conventional Scottish historiography was still stricken with inferiorism, and Nairn's account was simply, from one point of view, an extreme version, or *reductio ad absurdum*, of generally accepted beliefs and assumptions about the Scottish past (which can be crudely summarised as the view that, with the exception of a period in the eighteenth century, Scottish high-cultural history is a kind of void.).

The notion that the David Humes and Adam Smiths emerged, so to speak, from nowhere, and that after them Scotland ceased to have any significant intellectual culture, never had any real *a priori* plausibility. Total demolition of this perspective, and a revolutionising of our conceptions of Scottish cultural history, awaited the recent work of, among others, Alexander Broadie, David Allan, Alasdair MacIntyre and Cairns Craig. Whatever stories about the historical evolution of Scottish culture are accepted by future generations, the inferiorist version will not be one of them. But Nairn, it appears, has taken no interest in these re-appraisals. He does now concede, however, that his early polemics against what he terms 'the follies of tartanry' were excessive.

Commitment to a nationalist movement is typically bound up with beliefs about the worth of native traditions, and the value of a particular collective identity. No such beliefs are evident in the pages of *The Break-Up of Britain*: the attitude to Scottish culture and identity is here unwaveringly critical and hostile. Nairn had come to lend support to the movement for Scottish autonomy for reasons quite different from those motivating the mass of nationalists. Allegiance to the nationalist cause was justified as one response to 'the need of the post-war British left to discover... a way out and forward from its peculiar impasse'. Nationalism, in more specific terms, represented an escape route from the sclerotic state and politics of Ukania, a route whose final destination was socialism. That is to say, the achievement of Scottish sovereignty was not, in this argument, an end in itself, but the means to socialist ends, as this comment implied:

...in a Britain dominated by an England in transition to socialism, it goes without saying that (eg) Welsh or Scottish separatism would become—at least in their present form—dubious or backward trends.

The subordination of nationalism to socialist ends, together with the total absence of sympathy for Scottish cultural traditions which Nairn's writing displayed, made his position unacceptable to many nationalists. Nevertheless, it should be remembered just how radical and courageous a step it was in the kind of far-left milieux of the age where Nairn was a prominent theorist for anyone to embrace nationalism in the way he was prepared to do. In such circles the orthodox view was that nationalism was but one step away from racism and fascism, and thus to be combatted at all costs.

But the important point for the wider discussion is that Nairn's nationalism at this time was a form of what Neil MacCormick has called 'utilitarian nationalism'. In contradistinction to 'pure nationalism', the view that the Scots (or whatever nation) ought to form a separate state simply because they are a nation, utilitarian or instrumental nationalism justifies independence as an instrument for the achievement of other, *moral* goals (in the case of the form of instrumental nationalism endorsed by MacCormick, these are summarised as 'the well-being of the Scottish people').

Nairn's political argument, however, was soon to change in a significant way.

2.

Most of the essays comprising *Faces of Nationalism*, which contains the other major collection of Nairn's essays on Scotland and Scottish nationalism, were written after 1989, and in this work the prospect of any 'transition to socialism' understandably disappears. 'Socialism', Nairn now writes, 'has to find new, post-1989 bearings, although some will find this a charitable description of its plight.' He even declares, in slightly less Delphic mode, that uneven development is 'the only kind which capitalism allows', and goes on—'the kind which has finally, definitively established itself since 1989 as the sole matrix of future evolution', which seems to suggest, without quite wholly implying, that capitalism is now inevitable.

At the same time, Nairn's commitment to the cause of Scottish nationalism persists. But if the socialist argument for nationalism can no longer be plausibly invoked, on what grounds does Nairn now justify his political position?

We can begin to answer this question by observing that it is certainly not the case that Nairn's theory and assessment of modern Scotland and its culture have changed. About his unremittingly negative interpretation of modern Scotland, Nairn is unrepentant: on this front no revisionism is to be entertained. He refers to those who want to dispel what he calls 'the familiar notion of Scotland's being deformed or deeply defective in some way—a cripple or half-wit among the nations', and continues (in a remark which modestly understates Nairn's own role in making this notion familiar):

Speaking as one guilty of disseminating this libel in times past, I feel obliged to utter a few words in its defence.

Echoing the case made in *The Break-Up of Britain*, Nairn insists on the 'freak' nature of modern Scottish historical development, and writes, for example, that the choice of modernisation without nationalism makes Scotland an 'oddity in the zoo'. Divorced from the world of high politics, Scottish civil society became 'a kind of ailment, a practically pathological condition of claustrophobic, cringing parochialism and dismal self-absorption'. Special contempt is reserved for the Scottish institutional elites who are responsible for Scotland's being a 'decapitated' nation. They form, Nairn thunders, 'the unique Scots phenomenon of a national sub-mandarin class cringingly proud of its "responsible" addiction to political *coitus interruptus*.'. Not only has this 'stupefied provincial sub-establishment' failed to exercise proper leadership; its 'craintive moderation' and 'caution ' have 'permeated the nation'.

One implicit challenge to Nairn's reading which has received considerable attention is the argument presented by Lindsay Paterson in *The Autonomy of Modern Scotland*. Once an enthusiastic anti-tartanry crusader, Paterson has since absconded from the Nairnite camp, and in the text cited is guilty of the apostasy of contending that the political plight of modern Scotland may not have been as lamentable, after all, as nationalists believe. It is true, his argument goes, that since 1707 Scotland has not been in legal terms a sovereign state, but it has in practice in most important areas been run by Scots through institutions which are themselves distinctively Scottish. After comparing Scotland with other European nations in this regard, he concludes that 'By European standards Scottish autonomy was at worst normal, at best actually quite privileged'. It is therefore erroneous to regard Scotland's institutional bourgeoisie as having been and being a collection of 'abject', 'timid' 'dupes', who well deserve their 'reputation for craveness'; they are to be seen, rather, on Paterson's account, as sage political operators, or, in his own words, practitioners of 'sensible *Realpolitik*'. This is in Nairn's eyes true and unpardonable heresy. Paterson's defence of a national leadership class content to merely manage rather than actually rule Scotland is hounded mercilessly, and depicted as a eulogy to self-inflicted political castration, and acceptance of the 'unavowable curse' of an identity definable by the reflex of 'doing as you're telt'.

No-one familiar with Scotland could in honesty deny that Nairn's analysis here captures an important and uncomfortable truth about the national psychology. However, the argument against Nairn's theorisation of Scottish history was never that it fails to describe and account for aspects of Scottish reality, but that it leaves so many aspects of that reality out, and unaccounted for.

The reader of *Faces of Nationalism* cannot fail to note the prominence in the text of Nairn's sexual metaphors, or fail to grasp what they signify. The achievement of sovereignty would represent release from the condition of political emasculation, impotence, eunochdom Scotland has endured since 1707: the ability, at last, to experience political climax. It is all a question, in the end, of attaining virility, potency—of power. (Discussion of the question whether Nairn's politics and his account of national identity are 'gendered' in an unacceptable way can perhaps be left to feminist critics.)

Nairn has little patience with arguments that national identity is being rapidly superseded by sub- and supra-national (or, local and cosmopolitan) identities. Nor does he have any sympathy for the postmodernist emphasis on identity as a matter of choice, or the notion that in the self 'there are multiple or equivalently valid identities existing in no special order of significance', an idea he dismisses as 'a form of cant'—here he surely has a point: intellectual modishness notwithstanding, some form of 'essentialism' is unavoidable, since the realities of language and *habitus* cannot be escaped. The phenomenon of sovereign statehood continues to be an integral part of the functioning of real politics, he insists, and as long as other nations possess it, so should the Scots. The argument is thus simple, and it deploys, as Nairn states, 'no standard-issue nationalist rhetoric', the 'familiar motifs and incantations' of false-consciousness nationalism. Nairn has arrived, in fact, at an idiosyncratic form of what MacCormick calls pure nationalism. The Scots are a nation; *ergo*, they should possess a state, and exercise the same kind of power as other nation-states do. That is all. ('Idiosyncratic', since pure nationalisms typically invoke former national achievement and greatness to support the case for independent statehood.)

Although it may seem strange for a supporter of Scottish independentism to have such a negative view of the national culture as Nairn does, the theorisation of Scottish history and his political stance have never in reality been in tension, because 'standard-issue' nationalism (or national trumpet-blowing) has always been eschewed. In *The Break-Up of Britain*, the nationalist stance was adopted as an instrument of socialist strategy, not a matter of asserting one nation's culture, or some aspects of that culture. And in the position presented in *Faces of Nationalism*, the historical theory and the political argument have in fact been brought into alignment. For power as a nation rather than socialism is now the goal, and it is by achieving such power that we will overcome that curse of self-inflicted impotence that the theory has revealed to be at the heart of modern Scottish identity.

What Nairn's instrumental and pure nationalist positions have in common is one unfortunate feature—a form of elitism, for want of a better word—which an American commentator, Joan Cocks, has alluded to in these terms: Nairn brings nationalism to center-stage, explains it and defends it—but he does not believe in it. To see nationalism as intellectually false but historically right has convoluted political implications for the seer; the ability to be a nationalist is not one of them.

On the political ground, effective nationalism requires meaty fare, its characteristic 'motifs and incantations'. As Nairn insists, common-or-garden nationalism is Janus-like: it looks to an idealised national past, invokes a *mythistoire*, in its task of forging a better future, and thus involves 'cults of a particular past and tradition'. But Nairn himself of course is above such things as what in Nairnese are characterised as ancestor-worship and veneration of tribal custom. He is therefore in much the same position as those who, while not themselves believers, have thought it a good thing that others believe in God. Nairn, we might say, does not believe in the nation, but at the same time he is in favour of belief in the nation. False consciousness is good for you.

3.

Nairn has referred more than once in his published work to W.J.M.Mackenzie's book *Political Identity*, and borrows from it the idea that national identity is to be defined in terms of communal action. More recently, Cairns Craig, adapting John Macmurray's definition of the self as agent, has proposed a similar, 'performative' definition of a nation: it is an agent, it is what it does. There is in fact nothing new about such conceptions: the doctrine that the tree is known by its fruit is found in Matthew's gospel, and Augustine provides a performative definition of nationality when he writes that 'to understand the character of a particular people we must examine the objects of its love…'

Mackenzie actually puts forward two ways of making sense of the existence of collective identity. The first equates it with the presence of common purpose and action. 'A discussion of political identity is perhaps primarily a discussion of the conditions in which it is possible to realize "common purpose".' He also writes that 'The classics of political theory are about communality, about social entities, but only to the extent that they are or may be capable of purposive collective action'. So, it follows, statements about strong or weak identity, or about the breakdown of identity can be translated into equivalent statements about strong or weak common purpose and collaboration, or the breakdown of common purpose.

But Mackenzie is aware that as an account of national identity this is still too thin. His second approach appeals to language, but language in a very extended sense. It includes what he terms 'myth, symbol, ritual and ideology', the latter term covering also what he terms 'doctrine', or 'the attempt to ground logically and to expound systematically the meaning of a complex of myth, ritual and symbol'. These things are, he says, 'of extreme importance in the attempt to give a workable meaning to talk about social and political "identity" '.

The relationship between practical identity and what we might call discoursal identity is of course that, since action is belief-informed, the former presupposes the latter. Or as Mackenzie writes, 'conscious concerted action is not conceivable without channels of communication'. On this aspect of Mackenzie's discussion Nairn does not elaborate: he is understandably reticent about this stress on the importance of myth, symbol, ideology and doctrine in identity—understandably, since this looks dangerously like the territory occupied by standard-issue or false-consciousness nationalism (which, as we have seen, is for Nairn politically necessary, but of course specious). And one question which Mackenzie's discussion raises for us is therefore this: does Nairn's view of nationalism and nationalist debates rest on a serious misapprehension?

Nairn says that he has been 'permanently influenced' by the essay on nationalism in Ernest Gellner's Thought and Change (1964)—this piece is in Nairn's view 'the most important thing written about the subject in recent times (which actually means "ever")'. [personal communication] Gellner's theory—which has been criticised as a form of functionalism—stresses the exclusively modern character of nationhood, and the role of uneven economic development in the origination of nationalisms. The theory, or to be more precise the thesis it involves according to which nationalisms invent nations, rather than the other way round, readily fed into the 'invention of tradition' discourse which for a time was in vogue, and served as a useful tool to ridicule nationalism in the hands of those (like for instance Lord Dacre) intent on propping up the disintegrating Ukanian empire. It is true also that Gellner greatly enjoyed indulging a caustic wit at the expense of populist- or vulgar-nationalist scribblers—though he generously accepted that their enthusiasm, even if it was the fruit of delusion, was sincere, and not consciously driven by the material motive which, at least according to Gellner and Nairn, is the 'real', essential logic of nationalism. It is therefore all too easy to overlook or forget the facts that not only did Gellner challenge what had been a kind of liberal intellectual consensus that nationalism was a mode of political atavism, but also that he was in fact arguing that nationalism on the whole is A Good Thing. Marxist-socialist fantasies notwithstanding, it is evident that nation, or culture-bond, is dominant over class identity and loyalty (the effective political weakness of 'internationalism' is another Gellnerian theme which is echoed in Nairn's work); so the dispossessed in the peripheries would do well not to expect solidarity from the proletariat in the core, and should attempt to exercise what political control they can over the forces of development. Nationalism also serves to guarantee 'cultural diversification' (Gellner's rather cursory argument as to why this is desirable is that 'pluralism is some kind of insurance against both tyranny and political folly').

Nevertheless, according to this theory, as we have seen, the actual content of nationalist arguments—the passionate outpourings of the sincere but deluded propagandists who, as Gellner says, know not what they do—is of little or no intellectual interest (and of little or no political moment): as Gellner also writes, 'Their precise doctrines are hardly worth analysing'. Thus Nairn's theory of Scottish history, which finds nothing of value in modern Scottish culture, is reinforced by the theory of nationalism he adapts from Gellner in the conclusion that 'standard-issue' nationalist discourse (which takes this culture as its object), though it is functionally essential—some set of myths and delusions is required to fire the masses—is as far as its content is concerned unworthy of serious intellectual engagement.

Gellner wrote that a grave underestimation of nationalism was one of marxism's two main errors (the other being the thesis of increasing proletarian immiseration). But perhaps Gellner and Gellnerians like Nairn are also guilty of seriously underestimating *nationalism* in their view that the content of nationalist discourse is of no import.

This suggestion is made in a fascinating recent contribution to nationalism theory by Roman Szporluk (in John A. Hall, ed., *The State of the Nation: Ernest Gellner and the Theory of Nationalism*). Briefly, Szporluk's main argument is that nationalist movements are not in reality, as the Gellner theory simply seems to assume, monolithic, homogeneous, unified, and controversy-free. Within nationalist movements there are, typically, debates and disputes about the nature of national identity. Such movements involve, that is to say, a struggle over which idea or ideas of national identity, or, to put this in another way, a dispute or set of disputes about which aspects of national identity (which will include conflicting and contradictory moments) are to play, in the definitions of identity and of policies, key roles. In this process some conception or conceptions of national identity, or 'visions of the nation', become dominant, others are marginalised or discarded. 'National identity is a subject of intranational contestation', says Szporluk, and nationalist debates form 'a battlefield in the struggle for hegemony within the nation'. And to understand this is also, obviously, to understand that nationalist ideas and nationalist thinkers, *pace* Gellner and Nairn, do after all matter. Indeed, what Szporluk's discussion implies is that it is hard to think of what could matter more. Or, in Szporluk's wonderful ellipsis, 'philosophy *equals* nationalism'.

One influential 'vision of the nation' which has been propagated and contested in recent intellectual debates that concern nationalism is of course Nairn's own. An allied view is presented in a well-known study by Colin Kidd—*Subverting Scotland's Past*—, in which the Scottish past is depicted as ideologically bankrupt, useless as a source of ideas and values that could have relevance to present and future politics.

Certain other contributions can be read as critical responses to this position, and elaborations of alternative visions (which does not of course mean that their authors are to be necessarily identified as supporters of Scottish nationalism). We might mention as an example MacIntyre's sympathetic treatment, or, we could perhaps say, defence, of pre-Enlightenment Scotland in *Whose Justice? Which Rationality?*, a type of community, as he writes, 'which is understood by most of those who inhabit it as exemplifying in its social and political order principles independent of and antecedent to the passions and interests of the individuals and groups who compose that society...' And allied to this view are the attempts by William Storrar, Duncan Forrester and others to argue for the retrieval of a socially radical strain in the history of Scottish Christianity which is conceived as one element of Scottish identity. It is worth noting, in this connection, that in his study of Scottish nationalism, *Claiming Scotland*, the American scholar Jonathan Hearn emphasises that in much Scottish nationalist discourse there is an invocation of 'a national identity historically rooted in egalitarian values and opposed... to the values of... the unbridled free market', and a re-affirmation of the 'social bonds of common membership in a community... ' Hearn, here echoing the main point made by Szporluk, therefore takes nationalism (or at least Scottish nationalism) to be centrally concerned with what beliefs and values should base and shape the life of the nation.

What 'doctrines', to use MacKenzie's word, are we to hold, and what common purposes are they to inform? Or to put this in other words, borrowing from Augustine, what are to be the objects of this nation's love? To such questions Nairn's contentless nationalism provides no answers; but they are the questions that nationalism is—dare this be said?—'really' about.

R.D. Laing

Gavin Miller

The psychiatrist R.D. Laing was born in Glasgow, on 7 October 1927. He died, aged 61, on 23 August 1989, while playing tennis in St Tropez. Memorial services were held in London, New York, and other cities across the world. In the course of his troubled life, Ronald Laing moved from the forefront of humanist psychiatry to a position of notoriety. Latterly, he was alcoholic, professionally unlicensed, and as disturbed, at times, as anyone he had ever treated. His work also descended into near-madness—he declared, for example, that his problems could be traced to the hostility of his mother's uterus, eight days after he was conceived. It is hard to forget such a figure; but it is easy to overlook the enormous influence upon psychiatry of his early work and ideas.

Much attention has been paid to the psycho-biographical aspects of Laing's life. There can be little doubt that an upbringing such as Laing's would create either an outright madman, or an excellent psychotherapist. He seems to have been raised in the kind of family he would later come to analyse as amongst the causes of schizophrenia. He was an unwanted child whose mother concealed her own pregnancy, cut him off from friends and family, and required that her obvious dislike for the fact of her son's existence be regarded as maternal solicitude. But if this upbringing gave Laing a motive and material for his theories, it did not give him the intellectual skills to analyse his own experience.

To find the ideas which helped to create *The Divided Self* we must look beyond the personal context of Laing's life, and investigate instead the fertile intellectual milieu which fostered his talent. Much has been made of Laing's induction into the group associated with the neurosurgeon Joe Schorstein and the psychotherapist Karl Abenheimer. There can be little doubt of the consequent influence of European existential thought upon Laing: indeed, were it not for his national service, Laing would himself have moved to the continent to study under a colleague of the existential psychotherapist, Karl Jaspers. The existential school of psychiatry undoubtedly contributes to the ideas behind Laing's most important work, *The Divided Self* (1959). Laing himself insists that 'this book attempts an existential-phenomenological account of some schizoid and schizophrenic persons.' His basic argument is that psychiatry tends to see the patient 'as a complex physical-chemical system, perhaps with its own idiosyncrasies but chemical none the less for that; seen in this way, you are no longer a person but an organism.' It takes 'the language of existential phenomenology' says Laing, to appreciate that a person may be seen 'as a person or [...] as an organism' accordingly as he or she is 'the object of different intentional acts.' When a man is treated as an organism, 'there is no place for his desires, fears, hope or despair as such. The ultimates of our explanations are not his intentions to his world but quanta of energy in an energy system.'

Oddly, though, Laing's most explicit acknowledgement with regard to this distinction is not to an existential psychoanalyst, but to the Scottish philosopher, John Macmurray. As Laing puts it, Macmurray's philosophy attempts 'to *think* of the individual man as well as to experience him neither as a thing nor as an organism but as a person.' In works such as *The Self as Agent* (1957) and *Persons in Relation* (1961), Macmurray sets out to explain philosophically why human life cannot be thought of under objective categories, and why, indeed, the world of things is derivative of a world that is primarily active and interpersonal. Laing differs from Macmurray, though, in one significant area. In *Persons in Relation*, Macmurray argues that a psychiatrist must approach his patient with an objective attitude:

The behaviour of the neurotic is compulsive [...] The motives of his behaviour are no longer under intentional control, and function as 'causes' which determine his activity by themselves. This, at least, is the assumption underlying the change of attitude [by the therapist], the assumption that human behaviour is abnormal or irrational when it can only be understood as the effect of a cause, and not by reference to the intention of an agent.

Laing, however, would see this as a failure on Macmurray's part to consider the possibility that seemingly insane behaviour may, in fact, be intelligible, intentional agency.

Laing's psychiatry is unified by the idea that psychiatrists habitually preclude an understanding of their clients as intentional beings. Indeed, so ingrained is objectification in the name of 'objectivity' that our automatic temptation is to say that 'psychiatry' cannot understand its 'patients'. In fact, there is no psychiatry beyond the intentionality of practising psychiatrists; and 'patients' are not in fact patients, they are *agents*. In so far as psychiatrists do not see themselves as engaged in what Laing calls a 'study of human beings that begins from a relationship with the other as person,' then, *a priori*, they turn troubled persons into malfunctioning things. The behaviour of the client is now a matter of structural or chemical causes in the brain. The possibility that the client may be engaging in some kind of comprehensible intentional behaviour is automatically excluded.

Laing therefore argues that many of the seemingly incomprehensible utterances of the mad can be understood by a sufficiently sympathetic listener:

It is not uncommon for depersonalized patients [...] to speak of having murdered their selves and also of having lost or been robbed of their selves.
Such statements are usually called delusions, but if they are delusions, they are delusions which contain existential truth.

For Laing, these declarations express the despair of an individual who has never been able to realise her own spontaneous and autonomous life in relation to others. As a consequence, she has withdrawn from social being; her 'true' self is an inner, mental existence, concealed (for a while) behind a 'false' exterior self of compliant, embodied life. What seem to be bizarre utterances which could only be 'caused' not 'meant,' are attempts to express the loss of a vital relation to the social world.

Laing's argument may be generalised to more familiar examples of mental illness. Consider for example the distinction made between reactive and endogenous depression. The former is regarded as having some kind of external 'cause'—the death of a loved one, say—while the latter, in the absence of such an event, is regarded as due to some internal pathology. This distinction is, of course, facile. The difference is really between misery for which the doctor can find an intelligible reason, and that for which he cannot. The latter kind is regarded as 'malignant,' as 'pathological,' as if these were inherent qualities, rather than an admission of a failure of comprehension. There is indeed depressed behaviour which is wholly without reason—but the danger is in complacency over this distinction. Not so long ago, a woman who was miserable because she was a housewife with two children to look after might have been regarded as pathologically depressed—particularly if she was unable to explain why she should be so unhappy in her role. Who knows what other seemingly secure attributions of endogenous mental disorder may rest upon a similar insensitivity?

To Laing, the uncritically objective attitude to the madman is really a very ancient form of social exclusion. He discusses in his autobiography, *Wisdom, Madness and Folly* (1985), an incident in which the psychiatric staff with whom he works are offered buns baked by patients. The majority refuse. Laing remarks: 'Excommunication runs deep. A companion means, literally, one with whom one shares bread. Companionship between staff and patients had broken down.' There is no rational ground for the refusal to eat the buns; merely an irrational revulsion at the social meaning of this everyday ritual of communion. To eat the buns would be to break bread with the mad: but the mad, to the staff, are not kin with the sane; by virtue of their supposed neurological malfunctions, they are not acknowledged as fully human, intentional agents.

This archaic social distinction is one familiar from a tradition of Scottish thought which predates Laing. In his *Lectures on the Religion of the Semites* (1894), the Victorian social anthropologist, William Robertson Smith, discusses the rituals which establish group life. Pre-eminent amongst these is the communion meal:

> Among the Arabs every stranger whom one meets in the desert is a natural enemy, and has no protection against violence except his own strong hand or the fear that his tribe will avenge him if his blood be spilt. But if I have eaten the smallest morsel of food with a man, I have nothing further to fear from him; 'there is salt between us,' and he is bound not only to do me no harm, but to help and defend me as if I were his brother.

Those who are outside of such communion are aliens: they are subhuman; they are animals who resemble people. The psychiatric division between the sane and the mad, in its unthinking exclusion of intentionality from the disturbed, is a modern echo of an archaic distinction.

This *a priori* exclusion of the mad from recognition as intentional agents is central to most mainstream psychiatry. Every week offers some new discovery of the causes of mental illness. Scientists, the papers tell us, are confident of a certain genetic cause, or of the imbalance of certain chemicals in the brain. And yet, the fundamental objection remains: any human trait, or behaviour, can be given a strictly biological description. Schizophrenics may indeed, as studies have suggested, be born with an especially small amygdala-hippocampal complex. Yet that such a structure should be viewed as abnormal is entirely derivative of the abnormality encountered in contact with a schizophrenic. Without this primary experience of incomprehensibility, the correlative structure of the brain is merely an entirely neutral fact that is not, in itself, a disorder. If, however, a schizophrenic's behaviour should be comprehended then the search for a physical causality would be, in all senses of the word, impertinent.

The primary objectification of the mentally ill, which lies behind all natural-scientific investigation of madness, is the main object of attack for those who have followed (however unconsciously) in Laing's footsteps. For example, until 1973, the 'bible' of American psychiatry, the *Diagnostic and Statistical Manual of Mental Disorders*, classified homosexuality as a mental illness. This classification was discontinued due to social and political pressures from outside psychiatry. No scientist suddenly stumbled upon the unreality of this particular 'psychopathology.' Rather, as a result of political activism, a group whose behaviour had lead them to be excluded from society were now let back in. Their homosexual intentions were recognised, and no longer reduced to defective genetics, hormonal malfunctions, or wrongly conditioned reflexes. Now, even if today's genetics and neuroscience should discover a cast-iron distinction between homosexuals and heterosexuals, we should merely have an irrelevant fact. Similar political movements are now afoot to demand recognition of those who are excluded by a psychiatric diagnosis because, for example, they hear voices, or engage in some other behaviour incomprehensible to North American physicians. One can only hope that a new category of mental illness is not created in order to account for such defiant opposition to mainstream psychiatry.

This year sees the 75th anniversary of Laing's birth. It is a peculiar fact that, had Laing been a more successful human being, he would probably now be a more neglected figure. Students of Scottish culture tend to forget the achievements of quietly respectable thinkers. Laing's later life of notoriety, though, cannot be smothered by the usual cultural amnesia. Those who care to look into Laing's work will find insight and candour; and beyond that, an unfamiliar context of psychiatric and philosophical ideas developed by Dr Jekylls who had no Mr Hydes to ensure their lasting memory.

The Lockerbie Tragedy and the Limits of the Rule of Law in International Society

Anthony Carty

John Ashton and Ian Ferguson, *Cover-Up of Convenience, The Hidden Scandal of Lockerbie* Mainstream Publishing, Edinburgh and London, ISBN 1840183896 , 2001, pp. 400, £12.99

Introduction

The argument of this controversial but widely esteemed book is that irregularities abound both in the investigation of the Lockerbie crash and in the preparation and conduct of the trial at Camp Zeist. The book concludes with a call for an official inquiry which would address twenty five areas. These include the numbers and type of warnings received about the possibility of an attack; the number of bookings and reservations which were changed for the flight shortly before the tragedy; why Margaret Thatcher blocked a judicial inquiry called for by Cecil Parkinson; the involvement of the CIA and MI5 in hostage deals in the Lebanon around the time that scrutiny turned to Libya; the multiple involvement of the CIA with various stages of the forensic evidence and with actual or potential witnesses

These immensely complex issues of forensic evidence and investigative journalism are important. However, the intention of the present short essay around the book is to focus on the implications of specific aspects of the trial which the authors highlight in the closing chapters. These concern the quality of the evidence upon which Al Megrahi was convicted. It is well known that the evidence was circumstantial. However, opinions can differ as to how compelling an accumulation of such evidence can be. The essay follows the authors in its treatment of the judgement given by the judges at first instance in Camp Zeist. It is fairly obvious, on an actual reading of the judgement, that the judges were not convinced by the compelling character of the evidence that Al Megrahi was properly identified as the person thought to have planted the bomb. Nor does the court find any compelling evidence directly implicating him in planting it in Malta. They are not even convinced that the bomb must have been planted at Malta airport. While it is not ruled out as a possibility that Al Megrahi did plant the bomb the main impression that the trial leaves is that a very much needed effective response to the present epidemic of terrorism in international society may well not be recourse to the Rule of Law.

The Rule of Law supposes that a judiciary has effective institutional independence against the state. The judiciary must have sufficient power to extricate the information which it needs to form an objective factual judgement about matters in hand. It has also, of course, to be able to rely upon agreed normative standards which can be impartially applied. Finally, it has to be able to rely upon an executive to implement any decision to which it arrives, however reluctant the executive may be to do so.

None of these conditions usually prevail where issues of acute national security are deemed to apply. The idea of a threat to the security of the state and its population is itself so nebulous that judges do not have any effective criterion to apply. Human rights conventions always qualify their provisions in terms of the needs of national security. Apart from this, judges are, in the last analysis, officials of the state. This makes it difficult in practice for judges to force disclosure of information regarded as sensitive in terms of national security. At an even cruder level, it is inevitably difficult for judges, in an atmosphere of national crisis and even panic, to resist pressure from an executive which is, in terms of pure institutional weight, much stronger.

All of these difficulties are magnified at an international level. There is no compulsory international adjudication. The International Court of Justice is the principal judicial organ of the United Nations, but it functions virtually as an arbitration tribunal that states can go to as they wish. The UN Security Council is not required by any express terms of the UN Charter to observe any of its decisions nor even to enforce them if it does not wish to. The norms of international law are frequently vague and incomplete and the Court is not certain to have answers to face the present world crisis of terrorism.

In other words, what this short essay argues is that the Camp Zeist trial has to be seen in a perspective, both national and international, in which the judiciary is a very fragile institution in which not a great deal of faith can be placed. It is at the mercy of the pressures and tendencies to panic which an epidemic of any kind, not to mention terrorism, is likely to provoke.

What follows is a detailed consideration of a number of judicial cases to do with different forms of terrorism, with the Lockerbie Camp Zeist case placed in the middle..The depressing conclusion of the argument is that the Rule of Law affords us no protection or way out of the present crisis. In this sense, the essay endorses the arguments of *Cover-Up of Convenience*. The authors themselves may be suggesting at the end that somehow politically high powered independent inquiries might be more effective. Yet it is hard to see how they could enjoy impartial authority in the fragmented state of international society.

Court Adjudication of National Security Cases: The Legality of Nuclear Weapons, the Lockerbie Cases, and Regina v. Shayler (House of Lords).

The implication of a 'National Security-State' view of authority in international relations is that there is little to be expected from the possibility of an independent judiciary. Judges are, in any case, state appointees, whether at the national or international level. Even if an individual judge is independent in spirit, the power of a state apparatus in relation to an individual judge can only be overwhelming where the state considers that its national security is at issue. This is, in fact, reflected in judicial interpretations of the meaning of the concept of national security. The power of the state has, further, huge implications in terms of the access of the judiciary to the facts that could form the basis of an objective decision. A Court is not necessarily in any better a position to extract information from individual states than is a political body such as the Security Council.

1.   In The Legality of Nuclear Weapons Case (1997) the International Court of Justice decided that while the threat or use of nuclear weapons would be generally contrary to the rules of international humanitarian law:

In the view of the current state of international law, and of the elements of fact at its disposal, the court cannot conclude definitively whether the threat or use of nuclear weapons would be lawful or unlawful in an extreme circumstance of self-defence, in which the very survival of a state would be at stake.

Here is precisely an opportunity for the Court to interpret and apply general principles to a particular case. However, it preferred, perhaps correctly in terms of democratic theory, to accept the absence of state consent to a particular rule. This is, in effect, to accept a *non-liquet*, or, to fall back on the principle that what a state considers necessary for its defence is a matter for its conscience. The British judge, Higgins, dissenting, said that it was precisely the function of the judge to apply general principles relating to self-defence and humanitarian behaviour to develop an answer. Judges can elaborate the meaning of principles of general application in a particular case. The judge should decide between competing norms, for instance the practice of states relying on nuclear deterrence and rules that exclude indiscriminate and mass destruction.

The question is whether this means she should or can do any more than follow her own conscience. Higgins herself says that one has to remember that it is the physical survival of peoples which is at stake. She effectively comes down on the side of a right of self-defence, based upon the right of subjective assessment of the danger posed by 'the other'. The reason is that we live in a decentralized (read: anarchic) world in which we simply cannot be sure of the intentions of our neighbours, 'the others'. In her own words some states choose not to be parties to non-proliferation treaties '…while other non-parties have declared their intention to obtain nuclear weapons; and yet other states are believed clandestinely to possess, or to be working shortly to possess nuclear weapons…' What follows, from a liberal perspective, is a modest expression of opinion. '…It is not clear to me that either a pronouncement of illegality in all circumstances of the use of nuclear weapons or the answers formulated by the court best serve to protect mankind against the unimaginable suffering which we all fear…'

The liberal conscience experiences uncertainty and fear, but never a guilt rooted in critical self-reflection. Who invented the nuclear weapons and first used them?

2. The two significant aspects of the Lockerbie Case (Libya v. UK and US, 1992) which deserves mention are (1) the interference of the Security Council, in particular the UK and the US, in the operations of the International Court of Justice in the case which Libya brought against these two states, and (2) the further tendency of the Security Council to undertake judicial functions. These aspects serve to stress that at the international level notional divisions of constitutional powers (executive, legislative, judicial) will be overwhelmed by the power of individual states.

It is well known that UNSC resolution 748 (1992) imposing sanctions on Libya was adopted on 31 March, when Libya had already brought an action to the International Court under article 14 of the Montreal Convention, including a request for interim measures. The Court was obliged to accept the principle that the UN Charter had priority over individual conventions of international law. It has been well argued that it is very questionable whether the conduct of the Security Council is compatible with the UN Charter. Whatever the merits of the Libyan regime it is not surprising that it should refute the imputations of terrorism made against it and that it should offer to have the matter adjudicated peacefully before the International Court of Justice. The reasoning of the Security Council only makes sense if one supposes that it has already decided the guilt of Libya, that it is a terrorist state, deprived of the basic legal right to have the question of its guilt adjudicated by an International Tribunal, which it was willing to do. The Charter requires, in article 36.(3) that issues of a legal character normally be submitted to the Court. The issue is more obviously a matter of assessing the evidence of responsibility for criminal acts— (a state instigating terrorism through its agents), —than it is a question of determining a threat to international peace and security, given that the controversy is about a past event.

3. The Camp Zeist Case (2001)

It is difficult to argue, in the present space, the merits of the evidence upon which Al Megrahi was convicted, but one may note agreement that there is no direct evidence linking him to the terrorist act of planting a bomb on the Pan American plane. Instead there is supposed to be an accumulation of circumstantial evidence which is, in the end, taken to provide proof of guilt beyond a reasonable doubt. In the present writer's view the most troubling parts of the evidence are the following. The case containing the bomb was supposed to have been placed unaccompanied on a flight in Malta. This fact was later to be combined circumstantially with the fact of Al Megrahi's presence in Malta just before the flight. Of the placing of the baggage on the plane the Court says that if the bag was launched from Malta's Luqa airport the method by which this was done was not established by the Crown. The Crown could not point to any specific route whereby the luggage could have been loaded. The Court accepted that the practices of reconciling baggage to passengers and engaging in repeated head counts of passengers and boarding cards at the airport '…seem to make it extremely difficult for an unaccompanied and unidentified bag to be shipped on a flight out of Luqa… '

Al Megrahi's connection with the incident is based upon supposed evidence that he made a purchase of clothing in Malta shortly before the incident and that he made an unexplained trip to Malta the night before the flight which supposedly carried the case with the bomb. About the evidence of the shopkeeper witness, Mr Gauci identifying Al Megrahi, the Court gave a remarkable judgement:. It considered that the witness '… himself felt that he was genuinely correct in picking him [Al Megrahi] out as having a close resemblance to the purchaser, and we did regard him as a careful witness who would not commit himself to an absolutely positive identification when a substantial period had elapsed. We accept of course that he never made what could be described as an absolutely positive identification, but having regard to the lapse of time it would have been surprising if he had been able to do so. We have also not overlooked the difficulties in relation to his description of height and age…'

The accused had also been issued with a passport under a false name by the Libyan authorities, known as a coded passport. The Court said that there was no evidence as to why this was issued to him. It was used in 1988 only on the night of 20/21 December on a flight to Malta, leaving the next day to go back to Tripoli. The other time he came to Malta on 7 December 1988 he had traveled on his own passport. The comments of the Court are quite extraordinary:

…There is no apparent reason for this visit, so far as the evidence discloses. All that was revealed by acceptable evidence was that the first accused and the second accused paid a brief visit to the house of Mr Vassallo at some time in the evening, and that the first accused made or attempted to make a phone call to the second accused at 7.11am the following morning. It is possible to infer that this visit under a false name the night before the explosive device was planted at Luqa (?), followed by his departure for Tripoli the following morning at or about the time the device must have been planted, was a visit connected with the planting of the device. Had there been any innocent explanation for this visit, obviously this inference could not be drawn...

All that can be added to these remarks was that the second accused was found not guilty, making any association of the first accused with him meaningless in terms of the prosecution.

It seems clear that the world of terrorist trials is as mysterious as any metaphysical reflection on the nature of the universe. A judge can only decide a matter by following his conscience. Reading the judgement the present author does think it conceivable that the accused was guilty. He would feel a little uncomfortable about screaming at the judges that they have taken leave of their senses. However, one does not 'feel oneself' to be in the presence of deliberations which have a professional character.

In *Cover-Up of Convenience*, Ashton and Ferguson comment on the feelings of the judges in the following blistering terms. While the authors accept that the alternative explanations of the bombing are equally conjecture, they object that the Court is asking the world to believe the following scenario. Megrahi, a supposed airline security expert, had chosen to dispatch a bomb from an airport that not only carried out explosive checks on passenger baggage, but also physically counted the bags to be stored in the hold, to ensure that they matched the number recorded by the check-in counter. By putting the explosive on a plane to Frankfurt, rather than a direct flight to London, he ensured that the bag would be handled by more airports and Pan Am staff. Earlier, Al Megrahi had bought the clothes for the bomb-carrying suitcase in a manner that was bound to attract attention to himself, and had left the labels in the clothes, thereby maximizing the possibility of their remains being traced back to the place of purchase. He had then colluded in the preparation of a bomb incorporating a timer that was not only impractical for the task in hand, but also, to the best of his knowledge, was supplied exclusively to Libya by a manufacturer with whom he had close personal ties.

In short, the judges had accepted that one of the greatest terrorist feats of all time was carried out by one of the most reckless and stupid terrorists of all time....

The main purpose of this argument has been, consistently, that the liberal concept of the rule of law and of international law is fundamentally flawed by the subjectivity of the individualism which it is supposed to uphold. Therefore, the aspects of the extraordinary Camp Zeist Lockerbie case which are stressed concern the subjectivity of the assessment of the presence of terrorists, i.e. not to speak of the uncertainty of anticipating a risk of terrorist acts. However, more bitter comments about the case do, if true, support the general argument of the essay about the possibilities of law among states where issues of national security are in play within a liberal framework. H. Koechler (UN report on the Lockerbie trial, 2001) presents two points as decisive, the presence of political officials of the United States and Libya in the proceedings to the point where the independence of the Court appeared to be compromised, and the persistent withholding of evidence from the Court.

He comments that two state prosecutors from the US Department of Justice were seated next to the prosecution team and appeared to control which documents were released to the Court. There were cables in connection with a Libyan CIA double agent which were only partially released to the Court. Finally the Lord Advocate stated officially that substantial new evidence had been received from an unnamed foreign government in relation to the case. The content of this information was never released. And the requested specific documents were never provided from a unnamed foreign government. Koechler comments '...Amid shrouds of secrecy and "national security" considerations, that avenue was never pursued, although it was officially declared as being of major importance for the defense case...' This is a reference to the alternative conjecture that the bombing was done at the instigation of Iran in retaliation for the shooting down of an Iranian airliner by the US. It was carried out by an alliance of Syrian proxy groups in which a Palestinian group was to the fore and Hizbullah played an important role. Iraq's invasion of Kuwait meant that from August 1990 it became important not to upset the post-Gulf War apple-cart. So, only after 1990 did the 'fingering' of Libya begin.

4. Regina v Shayler (House of Lords, 2002)

The Shayler case clarifies another aspect of the relationship between the National Security State and human rights. Shayler published articles in *The Mail* on Sunday on 24 August 1997 in which he alleged that there had been

UK Security Service plots to kill the President of Libya and various other malpractices. He did this on the basis of material he obtained as a member of the Secret Services, although he published it after he had resigned from the Service. He was prosecuted under the Official Secrets Act 1989, which contained an absolute prohibition on members or former members of the Secret Service disclosing any information for whatever reason, excluding any public interest defense. The Act provided a very elaborate system of internal review to which a dissatisfied member of the Service could have recourse, including judicial review of the refusal of his superiors to act on his complaint or to allow him to disclose information.

Shayler himself made no use of any of the internal remedies available to him. So, it is difficult to see how he could not be guilty of an infraction under the 1989 Act. However, the interest of the case is the reasoning of the judges in the House of Lords. This indicates that there are probably no circumstances in which any member of the Security Services would have any reasonable prospect of preventing illegal behavior by the Secret Service despite the presence of internal appeal procedures and judicial review. The decision of the House of Lords is all the more important in that it appears to provide a convincing case that it has given full weight to the impact of the European Convention on Human Rights and that it is only following the usual European practice.

The House of Lords refers to the reasoning underlying the legislation (the 1989 Act). All disclosures by members of the Secret Service are especially damaging because they carry an obvious added credibility. They will reduce public confidence in the Secret Service's ability to behave effectively and loyally. Any trial procedure which had to consider the material disclosed would be bound to damage the processes whereby the information had originally been obtained. Such a trial would assist terrorism. The Secret Service would lose its usual option of leaving all statements about its activities unconfirmed, whether true or false.

In other words it is the rule of law/the judicial process which is itself incompatible with the demands of national security even in a democratic state. The policy of the legislation is that any attempt to insert a public interest defense would make it impossible to achieve clarity in the law.

The judicial comment on the Act is that a defendant cannot show that it was in the national interest to disclose the information. Nor may a jury so find. The judiciary does have a responsibility, if a matter comes up for review, to engage in a balancing act. It must apply a principle of proportionality that is more liberal than the traditional common law ground for judicial review. The difficulty is that there is thought to be no way of 'balancing' the following consideration. In the words of Lord Bingham:

> … If the information or document were liable to disclose the identity of agents or compromise the security of informers, one would not expect authorization to be given. If, on the other hand, the document or information revealed matters which, however scandalous or embarrassing, would not damage any security or intelligence interest or impede the effective discharge by the service of its very important public functions, another decision might be appropriate…

These are precisely the terms in which the executive usually refuses to take political bodies into its confidence. The irrelevance of the idea of law is made clear where Lord Bingham goes on to repeat the advantages of excluding a public interest defense.'…Otherwise detailed facts concerning the disclosure and the arguments for and against making it would be canvassed before the court and the cure would be even worse than the disease…'

Another judicial comment appears to be more critical of the 1989 Act. Lord Hope remarks that the defect of the Act is that it does not identify the criteria that officials should bear in mind when taking decisions as to whether or not a disclosure should be authorized. However, the tone of the judgement is once again in favor of the state. The scheme of the Act, the possibility of internal authorization, subject to judicial review, is appropriate. Lord Hope's reasoning is particularly interesting in the light of the comments which have been made of the Camp Zeist Case. What the public interest requires is, effectively, anybody's guess, given the fallibility and finitude of the human condition. That is why we need Leviathan. In Lord Hope's own words:

> …However well intentioned he or she may be, a member or former member of the security or intelligence services may not be equipped with sufficient information to understand the potential impact of any disclosure. It may cause far more damage than the person making the disclosure was ever in a position to anticipate. The criminal process risks compounding the potential for damage to the operations of these services, if the prosecution have to prove beyond a reasonable doubt the damaging nature

of the disclosures... And it has to be borne in mind that a successful prosecution will do nothing to remedy the damage that a disclosure of security or intelligence information may have caused. Damage already done may well be irreparable, and the gathering together and disclosure of evidence to prove the nature and extent of the damage may compound its effects to the further detriment of national security...

It is quite clear from all of the judicial pronouncements considered in this section that judges, who are, after all, state officials, cannot engage in a balancing of human rights considerations against those of national security. These issues invariably involve considerations that are, by the nature of the thing, beyond their grasp because they do not have access to all possible information. Hence, they will always feel that, in the circumstances, they have to accord the state authorities the benefit of the doubt.

Conclusion

It remains only to stress that there should be no cause for surprise if the Coalition against Terrorism, in particular the US and the UK, do not see the need to submit their actions to the rule of law.

For instance, the Taliban Government of Afghanistan refused to hand over Al-Qaida suspects and Osama bin Laden in the absence of substantial proof, which is normal in extradition proceedings. This did not stop the US and the UK. They convoked the Security Council merely to inform it of the steps they are taking under the cover of the inherent right of self-defence, recognized by article 51 of the UN Charter. Their explanation to the Council is that they were undertaking actions to prevent and discourage renewed attacks against them. This form of military force is quite simply reprisal, prohibited under the UN Charter. Yet the atmosphere of a terrorist epidemic makes it unlikely that states will be restrained by 'fine points' of extradition proceedings where these concern such a state as Taliban Afghanistan. And if the Lockerbie Trial at Camp Zeist is a herald for the future it is difficult to imagine that the international community will regard the rule of law as a very positive and reliable alternative.

The conduct of the war in Afghanistan and in particular the civilian casualties exceeding those of September 11, the killing of Taliban prisoners, the treatment of some of them as outside the law in the Guantanamo base in

Cuba (beyond both US federal law and international law), the special courts martial envisaged (rules on proof, absence of appeal, death penalty), are all understandable responses to the horrors of September 11. However, they also show that liberal legal culture is simply swallowed up in the crises of the national security state. It has no effective way of resisting it.

The tradition which has grown up in the West, at least in the course of the 20th century, of relying on nuclear weapons as the main means of defence and security is quite simply terrorist. This is undisputed. It represents Peace through a Balance of Terror. When the matter came to the International Court of Justice, the UK and US judges were emphatic that law could not question the absolute right of the state to have recourse to nuclear weapons as a final means of defense if it genuinely considered it appropriate. It is also established and common practice for western states to engage in covert assassination of foreign leaders and other figures. Our highest judicial authorities say that there are no conceivable circumstances where such conduct may be challenged by anyone in a position effectively to resist it.

In this context the tragedy of Lockerbie in Scotland appears, however unfortunately, to diminish in international significance. One can expect worse to come.

New Deal for the New Writer

Donald Ross

I looked at the clock above the wall full of Job Cards as I sat waiting for my name to be called for my first New Deal appointment, knowing the only talisman I possessed was the material I'd written while on the dole. The only external, social reflection of the work had been in the short period of self-employment I'd managed; was in the books and magazines where the fiction had ended up being published. That was all I had so I'd brought along some examples, they were in the plastic bag lying by my feet. I was, for the first time ever, prepared to show them what I'd achieved with my focus. Maybe they could 're-focus' me, make use of the energy in some way. Maybe my skills were 'transferable'.

My appointment had been for 10.30am. I'd been five minutes early. I looked at the clock and was surprised to see 10.45am. I thought about going back to reception to see what was up but decided against it, the interview before me had probably just over-run. I got up and walked around, scanning the rows and columns of cards with job descriptions on. At 10.55 I went back to reception. The girl was standing chatting. When she spotted me she smiled, said she'd be right back and walked off down to the rear of the Job Centre, turned right and vanished into the building's bowels. I took a seat. Twenty feet away, to my right and behind my back, I heard my name being mentioned. I turned to look. There were three women at a desk. One was saying,

'... Donald Ross didn't turn up for his New Deal appointment... should we... '

Uh-oh! I was up from the seat and headed towards them.

'Eh... I heard you mention my name. I'm Donald Ross. I've been here since twenty-five-past-ten... '

The two women who'd been standing at the desk walked off and I was left facing the one whose desk it was.

'You're Donald Ross?' this woman said, looking down at papers.

'Yes.'

'Who did you tell that you were here?'

'I went to Reception at 10.25.'

'Who did you tell?'

This woman still hadn't looked at me once. I turned around in the seat I'd taken, craned my neck toward Reception. No-one there. Then the girl who'd said she'd be right back crossed my eye-line, heading back to Reception.

'It was her,' I said, feeling like a Gestapo informant instantly, a quick weird sensation in the belly. Woman At Desk's eyes shot up sharply for the first time, not at me but over my shoulder to register the girl who was just arriving back at Reception.

'Don't you believe me?' I asked.

Woman-At-Desk surprised me by looking straight at me with a quick smile.

'Yes.'

I waited for an explanation or apology about my half-hour wait. It didn't come. Very quickly, the woman's demeanour, her whole way of talking and looking at me (or not), began to remind me strongly of the repeats of the 1980 documentary series made inside Strangeways prison I'd been watching recently... late at night on BBC2. I'd watched the documentaries with suitable horror, realising that there was an evil spirit to be witnessed in the prison governors/officers: the evil spirit of power being wielded just for the sake of it, like a psychological cudgel. Now this woman's demeanour, more than anyone else I'd come across in 17 years, on and off, of attending Job Centres, was giving me a clue that part of this New Deal ethos involved a deliberate return to that authoritarian stance which is based in raw power without the safety-filter of mercy or reason.

She gave me a card that said her name was Jean and she was my Client Adviser. Should that not be 'Advisor', I thought. She was staring hard at the computer screen I couldn't see from my seat.

104

'So, you've been unemployed for two years?' she said.

'No... eighteen months.'

She clicked on her mouse.

'Oh, right. And your last job was... '

She frowned impressively.

'... *writer*... '

She managed to pronounce the word like it was a synonym for clown.

'Yeah... I was self-employed.'

'And before that... oh, I see you were unemployed also before that, for...
'

She thumped the keyboard heavily twice.

'Eh... two years,' I said, hoping it would sound better if I said it. But she repeated right away,

'Two years.' Making it sound pretty bad, like I'd thought she'd manage to.

'And before that you were working at... What... ?'

'Yeah,' I said, 'it's a shop.'

'You were serving customers?'

'Well, I was supposed to be but I never actually did that. They just had me lifting boxes around for a month, then paid me off.'

She sniffed comprehensively.

'And before that?'

By now I was in shock because there had always been an unwritten Job Centre rule. They never cared about anything before your current claim period. They never dug back into your unemployment history like this. Because it didn't just make *you* look incompetent... it reflected badly on *them* for allowing such long-term Dolehead-ness. The rule had always been that, so long as your job lasted 28 days at least, when you came back to sign on again they pretended they'd never seen you before. All they'd cared about was you not being on their *long-term* records, at which point you became a statistic, a problem. So, if you vanished occasionally for at least 4 weeks, went off their system like a blip going off a radar, well... they welcomed you with the open arms (so to speak) when you showed up again. You only became a BOGEY, an enemy aircraft on their radar-screen, when you hit the 2-year point. Or, now it seemed, the 18-month point.

But this Jean was relentless, she was actually *taking it all seriously*.

'And before working at What... you were... '

'Her face hardened with shock.

105

'Unemployed for *THREE YEARS!* she intoned. I looked around the office furtively. Two staff members had the heads up at their desks like meercats sensing trouble. I felt trapped. No-one had ever pieced together my history like this. I'd thought that one of those years had been lost permanently when I'd moved from Aberdeen to Inverness in `95. I knew if she kept going back, before the 4 year university period she'd hit one end of, she'd find another 5 years... the 5 years after leaving school at 16... 5 years only broken by occasional jobs and a year at college getting 2 highers... the 5 years of murderous unemployment that had led me to the crisis-point of beginning to write fiction.

'And you have an honours degree in English?' she asked.

I nodded and reached in my plastic bag with a crafty hand.

'I've never done this before,' I said, 'but... the letter I got about the New Deal said you'd want to match my skills to a job? So... I've always kept this separate, but, today, I thought I'd show you this stuff I've done.'

I passed a copy of a book to her.

'See, I had a story in that one... that was published last year and sold in most countries of the world... '

She turned the book over.

'Yeah... we all got our names on the back... '

'How much were you paid for this?'

'Well, it was payment for that... and another couple of editors buying my stuff... that let me go self-employed in '99. I got £165 for the story in that book.'

She looked at me and, when she laughed, I felt a bit surprised.

'Eh... I brought this one in, too. Like I said, I've never told any Job Centre staff about this before but, you know, the letter I got seemed a bit encouraging so... I thought I'd see if you fancied reading a story that's actually set, partly, in this Job Centre... '

I was reaching in my bag for a copy of *Chapman* when she dropped the book she'd been holding with my name on the back. I watched it bounce. She turned back to the screen, clicking at the keyboard. My hand was frozen in the bag, holding the literary mag.

'Mr Ross, it's important for you to understand that you are now at the Gateway to the New Deal. Prior to this, you would have had to be unemployed for two years but, since April, that has reduced to 18 months. The Gateway period you are now entering may last up to four months, but no longer. At that point we would have to resort to a 26-week intensive activity period, the details of which are unavailable at present, as this is an entirely new measure unimplemented in Inverness as yet. But I'm sure it won't come to that. During the Gateway period our main focus will be to get you into work again and restore your self-confidence.'

I let go of *Chapman*, held the plastic bag full of books snugly against my crotch.

'During the Gateway period you can have access to a variety of measures including the Program Centre, Counselling, Careers Advice, Mentoring etc. But our main focus is to get you into work immediately.'

'Yeah. I know. I just thought I'd tell you about the writing because it's a positive thing, the only thing I've really had success with... maybe the skill is, you know, transferable?'

She was looking at her computer.

'I see you're down here for Writer, Admin Assistant, Retail Assistant.'

'Yeah, I just apply for whatever comes up. Local shops.'

'I'm going to add to that... 'and whatever job I can do'... alright?'

I nodded.

'It's alright if we give employers your phone number, isn't it? Sometimes we do that if a vacancy seems to match.'

I nodded again.

'I'll just check what's in at the moment,' she said, staring at the computer screen. She found six vacancies and gave me a big lump of application forms and envelopes. As I was going she asked if there was anything else and, automatically, my hand reached in my plastic bag, dug out the *Chapman* mag.

'I could leave you this, see if you... or anyone else who wanted... fancied reading the story. It's about unemployment partly. It ends up with a bit set in this office... '

She nodded at the desk between us.

'Well, you can just leave it there if you want.'

I placed it on the exact area of desk I thought she'd nodded at.

Over the years I'd applied for thousands of jobs, literally. I was long past the point where I'd waste money posting off 6 Job Centre application forms. I did one, though, since it was a 'new deal' I was getting. The next day I was working on the new novel when the phone went at ten and instinct told me it would be the Job Centre. I did 1471. Number withheld. A couple of times later in the day the same happened again, while I was writing about a supernatural character with a blend of human and animal characteristics.

Then it was the weekend, but on Monday morning the phone started going at 8.40am. It rang and rang. This went on every half-hour or so until 4pm. The next day was the same, starting at 9.30am, finishing at noon. At 2pm I turned up at the Job Centre for my New Deal appointment with Jean. Right away she says,

'Is your phone working?'

'Yes.'

'Well, I've been getting Jackie to phone you for days, trying to change your appointment time because there was a double booking.'

'Right.'

'Are you sure your phone's working?'

'I think so.'

'Well, I'd have it checked.'

'No. It must be fine. I've been getting calls each day from people. But I'm out a lot, you know?'

'But we were phoning early, even this morning.'

'Yeah, I was out early yesterday and today. I like to go for long walks.'

Then the hard stare came, brown eyes behind specs, a certain anger. She was going to have to get me on something more concrete than that. She gave a heavy sigh and turned to her computer. I adjusted my neck to an angle that felt very innocent.

'Have you sent off those six forms yet?'

'Yes.'

'Have you heard anything back?'

'No.'

She sighed heavily again. I cleared my throat very loudly.

'Have you thought any more about the Counselling, Careers Advice, Mentoring or other options that are available to you in this Gateway Period? I assume you've been to the Program Centre.'

'No, I haven't.'

She looked shocked.

'What, and you've been unemployed for 18 months!'

'Well, I know two people who worked there as tutors until quite recently. They told me it was a waste of time... a rip-off... that the Centre gets people in because the government pays them for each person... but once you're in it's just a waste of time.'

'You're sure the reason you don't want to go isn't that you know the Program Centre has a good record of getting people into work?'

'No... I just wouldn't choose to go there. Is it compulsory?'

'I'm going to give you a fortnight to find work. At that time, if you haven't, it will be compulsory. I'll just enter that.'

Her fingers clattered on the keys. She went on at me for another hour, found me seven more jobs to apply for.

'What I really want you to focus on now and think about before our next meeting is part-time cleaning work. Perhaps the possibility of combining two part-time cleaning jobs.'

'Can I ask something? See the letter I was sent? It said that the New Deal would be helping me find the job I wanted, that would suit my abilities and qualities. That's why I showed you the books and talked about the writing. My mum's done part-time cleaning jobs for the last twenty years. I'll do whatever work I have to. But what I'm focussed on is the writing. And that letter, for the first time, it seemed to be seriously looking at what I'd be *useful* for. I mean, I've been to so many places like the Program Centre... or Restart Courses that, if you can already write a letter or CV, are just a waste of energy. But there must be some use somewhere for what I can do.'

'Yeah. I see what you mean. But, that letter, it's just the form letter that goes out. It's targeted really at 17-year-olds who don't know what they want to do. In your case, I don't even think Careers Advice would be useful because you already know what you want to do... writing.'

'But I could maybe *transfer* that ability to something else... '

'That's something you could discuss with a counsellor or a mentor. I'd advise that, to build your confidence.'

'But I am confident, about the work I've done, the books.'

'Confidence about meeting people face to face, though. Like in an office. Would you be comfortable in an office environment?'

I looked around, saw meercat heads pop up behind big desks.

'Not really.'

'Well, that's something you could talk to a Mentor or Counsellor about. That's what this Gateway Period is for. To help you. Although I must warn you, the Gateway Period can last up to four months but, if I feel you're not making use of its opportunities and nothing's being gained, you can be put immediately onto the 26-week Intensive Activity Period.'

'And you don't know yet what the details of that are?'

'No. But I could show you what we have been told.'

She got up and went to another desk, brought back a thick folder. I leafed through it. Timetabled days and weeks, 9am to 5pm it looked like, every day mapped out like the Restart Course from hell. Forget about having any brain left for a novel at the end of that lot.

'When you go on that you don't sign on any more. You're no longer on the Unemployment Register.'

'Right.'

'So, you can see, it's better if you get work... any work... in this Gateway Period. And, to stay in the Gateway Period, you have to make use of things to help you like the Program Centre, the Counselling, the Mentoring... '

'Right.' I nodded, still looking at the Intensive Activity folder. 'I see.'

'Do you need clothing, for an interview?'

'No. I'm still OK for clothes. Got stuff I never wear any more that I could use for an interview.'

An ex-girlfriend had spent three years kitting me out with clothes that felt too posh for me to wear in daily life. But Jean was looking at me with her Good Cop face... the Bad Cop having melted away somehow.

'If you need clothing, for an interview or a job, you're entitled to £200 in this Gateway Period. You don't have to have the interview or job already. You can choose clothes, anything you yourself would feel comfortable in, and we'll give you vouchers for up to £200 on the same day you find the clothes you want.'

So, Jean was ignoring that I'd said I didn't need the clothes. It reminded me of the Restart Course I'd done five years earlier, at this Program Centre she wanted me to go to. I'd turned up on the first morning absolutely soaked, drenched with rain, like a dripping rat. I'd been sitting in a chair, a puddle forming at my feet, drops plopping off my nose onto the table. And the woman there had asked me,

'Did you come on the bus?'

I'd looked at her in disbelief until she said,

'... because, if you *came on the bus*... you just sign here and we pay your travelling expenses.'

So then you're supposed to nod and say,

'Oh yeah, right, yeah, *I came on the bus*... '

and they give you the money. Which would be fine, except it lets them play Good Cop... until it suits them to play Bad Cop again.

Jean kept going on about the clothes, her demeanour very friendly.

'Just come in any time,' she said, 'even if you don't have an appointment.

110

And, if you see clothes that you'd like, we'll help. That's all we're trying to do, you know?'

She smiled. When the interview was over I stood up.

'Can I have the eh... '

She reached right away towards a pile on her desk. Dug the *Chapman* mag out of the bottom of the pile, handed it over. She'd known what I'd meant that quickly so it must have been on her mind. But she said nothing about it. I didn't ask if she'd read it or shown it to anyone else.

At the next interview her focus seemed to be shifted off the Program Centre. She just seemed keen to keep offering me the clothing £200. And to fix me up with a mentor and a counsellor. She kept telling me they wanted to help, to get me into work so I'd 'feel more confident'.

'Do you feel more relaxed with the New Deal now?' she asked.

I just looked at her. I'd learned that it was possible to get on with her as long as you let her play Good Cop about the £200 and as long as you didn't speak much... or even move. She'd have probably been really happy administering the New Deal to a stuffed animal. A stuffed animal in need of a shirt and tie. Although she did stress,

'But if you'd be more comfortable in jeans and a T-shirt, if that would make you more at ease in some sorts of interview... you know, we had a guy in yesterday, he had an interview today and he was in a panic to get clothes, so he went to Burton's and chose what he wanted. He was back here and I had a voucher made out for him in 5 minutes! That's how easy it is, Donald!'

She was beaming at me. Should I risk a nod? I risked it and it seemed to be of some use to her. She beamed harder.

Then she mentioned the £100 Job Grant.

'What? I'd get £100 just for signing off?'

'Yes. You just tick this box when you sign off, stating that you expect your job to last at least 5 weeks. The computer sees the tick in the box and the payment is automatic.'

'Would I get that if I was self-employed again as a writer?'

'I think so. I'd have to check with the girls.'

'The girls?'

She nodded to a desk across the office.

'The girls over there work for the DSS, not the Employment Service. I'll check with them.'

While she was over with them I did the calculations. Yes, I could manage it, that £100 was all I needed to put with payments from three editors. If I added £120 I'd saved I'd be able to manage a 3-month self-employment period, living on £25 a week, half what I got on the dole. I'd be able to re-draft my new novel! Jean arrived back.

'The girls say it doesn't matter what the job is.'

'So... I'd just enter myself as employer... and tick that box?'

'Yes. At least that's what the girls say.'

Before I went, Jean asked me if I'd have a serious think before our next meeting, about the Clothing Allowance, the £200.

But, the next time, she seemed excited about a new project. I'd decided to go along with whatever she wanted now, because I'd worked out that I could escape at any moment, go self-employed and fly away free. Also, an editor had suggested I do a piece about the New Deal itself, so the more I put up with the more I'd know. Now Jean was so intent on a 3-day Basic Employability Course that a local company was offering, she forgot all about the clothes and the Program Centre.

'I'd like a decision about Mentoring and Counselling, Donald,' she said. 'I think you'd find it very useful, to talk about what the barrier is between you and work. I mean, I can see, just looking at you, that there's no reason you should be unemployed. And I feel strongly that you should take the opportunity of this course. It will raise your confidence. They'll do mock interviews and other exercises. And I'd like you to try and use it as a way of helping you focus on the part-time cleaning work we talked about.'

The course seemed to have blown away the Program Centre idea.

'OK. I'll try this,' I said. She looked pleased. I risked a blink but she sniffed and straightened up in her chair so I returned to my stuffed bear impression. If you showed any sign of being alive, let alone 'confident', it didn't seem to fit her view of a long-term unemployed grunt and she turned into Bad Cop again.

'Would you like to wait until after the Course then, before you decide about mentoring and counselling?'

I nodded gently.

On the Wednesday morning of the Basic Employability Course I was up and out, walking towards town in the sunshine. I had the old plastic bag swinging from one hand, full of those books and magazines with my fiction in. I found the big stone building outside the Railway Station, checked to see what floor World Management had their office on. When I entered the room I sensed the old atmosphere again, that smell of Jobplan Workshop/Restart

Course/CSV/Jobclub. The tables, the whiteboard with the pens, the video/ TV on its metal stand and... yeah... the tea area full of upside down mugs. Five years and nothing had changed except I was older. But I looked around the room, saw that I was probably the youngest, that probably only three of us were under fifty. And no women.

The guys doing the course seem friendly, lively; one with a beard and ex-teacher aura, the other quite fit and quick looking. I'm helping myself to the tea when a big, white-haired guy comes over, says,

'Load of fucking shite, eh?'

I laugh, take a seat at a table, sip from my mug, wait. The guys doing the course stand up, introduce themselves as Greg and Jack. But right away the big, white-haired guy at the other table says,

'What's this all about, eh?'

He looks to be in his fifties. Then another man the same age, wearing denim and glasses, looking tough like a character in a Sam Peckinpah western, starts saying in an almost-shouting voice,

'I never fucking wanted to come here anyway! But they said they'd stop my fucking money! I'm no doing nothing, though! I'll sit here and that's fucking it.'

Greg and Jack are taking it well, laughing it off, doing a good job of not getting confrontational. Somehow they got us into doing an 'ice-breaking' exercise. You asked your neighbour five questions about himself, then he asked you. When we'd all done it we took turns telling the group about the other man. I said,

'Eh... this is Bill Kerr, he's worked for 8 years at the BBC in London, then 10 years at the BBC in Glasgow, as a sound engineer. Then he worked in Dingwall for 20 years, repairing electrical equipment until that business went into receivership and he was made redundant. Now he's been unemployed for 18 months.'

'Yes,' said Bill, "I never ever expected to be unemployed. It's been a shock. And I'm not getting benefit, you know. I was silly and told them what savings I had. So I'm only getting my stamp paid.'

'And they still made you come here?' said the wild Peckinpah cowboy from the other table.

'Aye,' said Bill, nodding and smiling.

Then Bill read out stuff I'd said about the writing I'd done. The other two at our table were an ex-painter and decorator/funeral attendant/*Monarch of the Glen* extra from Invergordon and a man who looked even more like a Peckinpah cowboy, but one built like Santa Claus. He was an ex-social worker/ published poet/professional storyteller/gold miner and pearl diver who'd worked in Afghanistan, India and California. At the other table there was a joiner; and the big, white-haired man who'd spoken to me first, he said he'd always just done whatever work there was going, but that work wasn't there any more, people were all into computers and things now. The other wildman with the specs didn't want to participate and no one tried to make him. Anyway, you could sense his Outlaw presence instantly, you didn't need to ask for credentials.

'I just want to check,' said Jack, 'did I hear someone say they hadn't wanted to come today?'

'That's right,' said The Outlaw, 'they told me my money'd be stopped if I never came!'

'Aye,' said The Storyteller, 'that's what I was told.'

Everyone was nodding. Jack shook his head and tutted.

'I had no idea they were telling you you had to come. This course should be strictly voluntary.'

There were grunts from both tables.

'And now you have to stay or you'd lose money. I see. Well, we'll try to make it enjoyable for you, now you're here, alright? I'll just go through to the office. Help yourself to tea, if you want.'

The Storyteller started asking about the writing so I got a book out of the plastic bag, showed it round the table. He asked if I had more so I was digging out copies of *Northwords*, which he said he'd had poems in himself.

'I've just sold a story to *The Scots Magazine*,' he said.

He recited a poem from memory that had been in *Northwords*, about bats and cricket and World War One fighter pilots. It sounded perfectly done, the poem. Then he was showing us his ring that he'd prospected for the gold and even made himself. He said he'd learned that in Scotland as a boy... how to find gold and make rings.

'In Scotland?' said Bill, amazed.

'Oh aye. I made a ring once with a pearl I'd fished for myself. But I had to get a man to set the pearl. I couldn't do that myself.'

When Jack got back from the office I saw him notice all the strange books and magazines that were littered now on our table. He handed out an exercise for us to do. I concentrated hard on it, got it wrong. The Storyteller was arguing with Jack on every point, fighting the system hard, like with a different persona from the one he'd used to tell about the ring and the pearl. The Outlaw was sitting, swearing. A second exercise was handed out. I dived in, did it wrong as well. It made you wonder if you were as clever as you thought you were. Then there was a break. Jack came over, kneeled down by our table, asked me about the writing. I showed him the books and mags. Couldn't stop myself saying the bit about,

'That book was sold in most countries of the world... '

'So you write stories?'

'And novels.'

'What... full length 300-page books... ?'

'Well, my new novel's 220 pages. I've got a literary agent. She's trying to sell it... and another novel I did... and a story collection. I'll be going self-employed again soon, with the money from a couple of editors buying stuff.'

I didn't tell him about my role as undercover New Deal reportage writer.

'Eh... ' I went, 'so you didn't know people were being made to come on the course? Or that it was being used as part of the New Deal?'

'The New Deal?'

'Aye. That's what I'm on.'

'And me,' said The Storyteller, then the ex-decorator.

'I'm just getting my stamp paid,' said Bill.

'No,' said Jack, 'I had no idea about any of that. It'll need to get straightened out. We're a private management company and recruitment service. We're nothing to do with the New Deal.'

The Storyteller started laughing like Santa Claus.

'You are now!' he said.

By the end of the first afternoon we'd done more exercises and watched a video. Before we went, Jack asked,

'Did you come on the bus?' and I thought, why not?

I made a claim for a £1.60 return journey. That'd get me £4.80 for the 3 days. We were all given envelopes. Mine felt heavy so I assumed they'd paid the three days in advance.

The next morning we were introduced to Jimmy, their IT manager, and put in a room full of computers. The Outlaw refused straight away to participate.

'I'm no fucking touching that thing. No me. I'll sit in front of it, like, but I'm no interested.'

'You'll maybe not find it so bad when you've had a go,' said Jimmy.

'No man. No fucking way. I'll just sit, though.'

'Look, if you won't take part you'll have to leave. I'm not having you sitting here doing nothing.'

It was edgy for a moment, then the ex-decorator said,

'Just give it a wee go, Tam. Nothing to lose, eh?'

'Aye, well... ' said The Outlaw and took a seat.

Jimmy started us with basic typing in of words, our names. Then he had us on a drawing/painting program. Copying a lorry he'd done on the big whiteboard. Then we were all doing giraffes, from memory or imagination if memory failed. Then colouring them in yellow, adding mustard patches. At the break the ex-decorator asked to read the story I had in the book that was sold in most countries. When Jimmy saw him with it he asked questions, then took a shot of the book himself. Five minutes later he came back in, sat down.

'You compressed it, didn't you?' he said.

'Well, it used to be chapter 3 of a 23-chapter novel. So it's an extract that I think of now as a story.'

'Aye, but you compressed it, no?'

I thought he'd not understood.

'Well, it's just that it was part of a bigger thing... '

He grinned.

'No, I mean the chapter itself, it used to be longer in itself, didn't it?'

'Yeah... ' I laughed, 'I'd forgotten that. That chapter was originally 3600 words... I chopped it down to 2400 so it'd have a better chance of getting space in that book. I'd forgotten I'd even done that. No-one's ever noticed that before, as far as I know, and quite a few have read it.'

'Aye, I knew you'd compressed it. It works. But it sets a breathless pace. You'd never be able to do a whole book like that. The reader would need more air to keep going.'

I was laughing.

'Aye,' he said, 'I do a lot of reading.'

'Right, do you fancy checking this one out? It's short.'

I gave him a copy of the *Chapman* that I'd left with Jean in the Job Centre. Ten minutes later he walked up to me, laughing, play-punched me in the gut.

'Aye, good one, Donald. Autobiographical, I think!'

'Aye, except I'm not a large brown bear... '

Back in the other room The Storyteller was reading a story I'd brought in to show him, one accepted for future publication, about brothers during World War One. The Storyteller had refused to take part in the computer session. He caught sight of my CV, saw I'd worked in Oklahoma and Ohio a few years earlier.

'I worked for a year on a ranch in Southern California,' he said. 'Used to go to the same bar Clint Eastwood was in a lot. One day I was sitting nearby, couldn't help overhearing. Eastwood crushed a beer can in his hand, said to the guy he was with, You know, I love the feeling of power that gives me. I never saw Eastwood in the same light after that.'

'Well,' I said, 'I think it's the work you should judge him on, not something like that.'

'What do you think's his best work?'

'Well... *White Hunter, Black Heart* maybe.'

'Who's your favourite director?'

'Eh... Sidney Lumet maybe. For *Equus... The Offence*.'

'Yes, *Equus* is very powerful,' agreed The Storyteller.

'When I was at the BBC,' said Bill, smiling as always, 'I was blamed one day for a mistake with the lighting and, afterwards, Raquel Welch came up to me and said that it wasn't fair, that it wasn't my fault. She thanked me for my time. I've always thought that was very nice of her.'

The Storyteller seemed uninterested.

'How old was she then, Bill? What year was it?' I asked.

'Oh, early 70s. 1972, I think.'

'Wow,' I went, 'vintage Welch, eh?'

At the end of the day Jack handed out travelling expenses envelopes again, gave me one with another £4.80 in it. I had a pang of guilt, then worked out that I'd be able to clear a total of £14.40 from the 3 days, if the same happened the next day.

On the third and last day everyone seemed to have run out of energy. We sat around for a while, drinking tea. The Outlaw had dropped out and the white-haired man was telling me that when he'd turned sixty his dole had gone up twenty pounds a week, with no explanation.

'You know what I think it is,' he said, the eyes narrow and sly, 'I think it's them saying, Right... that's you... you'll never be getting a job again so we'll give you this if you keep quiet.'

We were all sent to the Job Centre, asked to come back with the details of two jobs we'd like to apply for. I chose a couple of shop jobs but when Jack saw he said he thought it'd be more productive if I focussed on something to do with the writing.

'Well, I could write letters to a couple of publishers about the new novel I've got.'

'Right, would you need to go to the library today then, to get addresses?'

'No. I know these addresses by heart.'

Jack was laughing.

'Ok then. Do a couple of letters. Let me have a look, then we'll get them printed out in the office for you.'

When we'd all done our letters and given details so the office could print out CVs for us, we were all sitting and waiting to take our turns at the only things left to do. First, Greg took us out of the office and across the road to another office, one at a time, to answer questions on a computer that told you what job you should be doing. Then it was time for an individual interview with Jack, sitting in a small room and getting the forms filled out for admin purposes. When I saw he was filling out the form that would be returned to the Job Centre I said,

'Look, maybe I should tell you, the Job Centre sent me here so it would help me get focussed on part-time cleaning jobs... '

I'd seen that Jack was filling out the form, saying that the course had resulted in me writing letters to the two publishers and he was stating my Overall Employment Objective as 'Donald finding a publisher for his new novel.'

'See,' I said to him, 'I don't mind what you write because I'm about to go self-employed again. But I know that form's going to go straight to this woman called Jean and she's not going to like it being about writing, instead of the part-time cleaning jobs she wants me to focus on... '

Jack put down his pen and held his head in his hands.

'*Noo!*... they're really saying that to you? I'd argue against that all day... '

I blinked.

'Yeah,' I said and did a short laugh, 'thing is, though, if you want them to send more people to you... on the New Deal... they might not like all that stuff on the form, about the writing.'

Jack straightened up, shook his head.

'No, I'm happy to leave the form as it is... as long as you're sure you'll not get any trouble... '

'No. I'm safe now, with the self-employment.'

Jack signed the form, passed it to me. I took his pen and signed it, a quick shot of Jean's outraged face flashing across my eyelids.

'I always think,' said Jack, 'that you've got to stick to the high ground, do what you know is right.'

Back in the main room I told Jack I'd been having trouble getting the novel converted to Word, from the mad language of my stone-age Olivetti machine. Jack said that Jimmy would have a go at the conversion. If that didn't work he promised they'd scan the manuscript onto Word for me.

Before I left, I accepted the third envelope containing £4.80 'travelling expenses', bringing my profit for the 3 days to £14.40.

Maybe I should have tried the Counselling or tried to get a Mentor but, when I turned up to sign on the following Tuesday, all I wanted to know about was the £100 Job Grant. I was glad it was this nice girl, Susan, I was signing on with and not Jean. Susan went across to 'the girls' like Jean had done.

'Yes,' she said, 'they say you're definitely eligible for the £100. All you have to do is tick the box.'

Later that day I was crossing the bridge and passed Jean. I smiled and gave her a big Hello. Her eyes widened as she said hello back.

I started the self-employment, waited weeks for the £100 Job Grant.

When it didn't come I wrote a clinical letter, told the Job Centre Manager I'd been asked to write about the New Deal, that I'd be naming the Job Centre, herself and all the staff who had lied to me... if I didn't get the £100.

I got a letter back, telling me it was being looked into.

Then I got a £100 cheque, dated on the same day as they'd received my letter threatening to name them.

I re-drafted the novel during the 3 months self-employment and used the £14.40 'travelling expenses' from World Management to buy copies of *Macallan Shorts 4* and Canongate Prize's 'Original Sins'; trying to suss out the competition. One Saturday morning the disk came from Jimmy at World Management, the novel successfully converted to Word, and a letter from Jack saying he'd like a copy to read. It was good to know that New Labour's New Deal could work so well for the new writer.

Dislocating the Nation: Political Devolution and Cultural Identity on Stage and Screen

Ellen-Raïssa Jackson

The last decade has seen the rapid growth and acceptance of postcolonial theory in the academy, but this has been accompanied by continued debate, both among postcolonial practitioners and those committed to different theoretical standpoints, about the nature and scope of the term 'postcolonial'. After some initial resistance, Irish writing has generally been accepted into the body of postcolonial writing, largely through the work of theorists such as David Lloyd and Luke Gibbons, as well as through polemical projects such as Field Day. However, whilst many non-Irish thinkers are happy to consider Ireland as 'postcolonial' the response from within Ireland itself has been mixed. In particular, writers and academics from Northern Ireland have suggested that the postcolonial label assumes a homogenised Ireland that makes no distinction between the Republic and the North. In addition, critics like Edna Longley argue that postcolonial readings are often reductively nationalist and fail to respect or acknowledge Protestant and Unionist values and experiences. Similarly, Scotland has tended to suffer from an inability on the part of postcolonial critics to disaggregate Britain to the extent that one of their earliest and most important texts, *The Empire Writes Back* (1985), refers to Scotland in passing as 'in complicity' with the Imperial project and therefore worthy of little consideration.

Although Scotland has received little attention from postcolonial critics, a few readings of Scottish history and Scottish writing in a colonial context have been offered, most notably by Craig Beveridge and Ron Turnbull, Robert Crawford and Willy Maley. In the main however, postcolonial readings have been resisted or overlooked in Scotland. At best, the core-periphery theories that underpin early postcolonial readings have been used to explain the troubled and troublesome relationship between Scottish and English cultural production. In recent years, postcolonial theory has begun to question the dominance of the core-periphery model, which tends to focus the colonial experience exclusively on the relationship with the colonising centre. Critics such as Elleke Boheme and Bart Moore-Gilbert have called for greater consideration of transverse forms of anti-colonial collaboration and further study of the relations between different colonised nations and regions. The challenge that postcolonialism presents to existing critical frameworks is matched by the reluctance of critics to read Scottish and Irish writing against and alongside one another. Whereas a strong urge to bring together cultural analyses of Scotland and Ireland has been shown in projects such as the Irish-Scottish Academic Initiative, the debate surrounding the New British History, and through suggestions in the work of Robert Crawford, Marilyn Reizbaum and Seamus Deane, an equally forceful rejection of this approach has surfaced in the work of Fintan O'Toole, Colin McArthur and others. The reasons for this divergence of opinion are not only explicable in terms of the politics of the Republic, Northern Ireland and Scotland, but are caught up in questions of canons, cultures and critical perspectives. To some extent, such divisions are neither novel nor surprising and strong parallels exist in the complementary debates in Scotland and Ireland about the direction a national literature should take on the threshold of the twenty-first century.

However, more recently, all things Irish and Scottish have experienced a second revival—a boom in popularity that has exposed a body of talented writers to international critique and acclaim. Similar to the first revival, the new Irish fiction that wowed Britain and America in the late 1980s was followed by an upturn in interest in Scottish writers in the early 1990s. Without dismissing the value that the confluence of such interest may hold, it is worth bearing in mind that the labelling and marketing of Irish and Scottish culture can homogenise and stifle any creative effort that identifies itself with the nation. In the conclusion to his book on the Irish novel, Gerry Smyth suggests that 'it may be that "The New Irish Fiction" is little more than an invention by a loose affiliation of London publishers, creating a critical category (and a market) where before there was only a set of vague impressions' (The Novel and the Nation, 1997). Similarly, the boom in the market for Scottish fiction has tended to depend upon individual books creating an impression of what could be called 'Kelmanism'. Cultural products that do not fit the mould are, at best, criticised for their failure to do so and, at worst, completely ignored.

There are many reasons why both Scottish and Irish culture might be experiencing a boom in popularity, particularly in Britain and America. Yet, however valuable such interest may be, it has repercussions in the form of a heightened antagonism between Scotland and Ireland, who compete for a similar share in the cultural market. This is particularly true in the case of the film industry, where tax incentives and Government co-operation, following the radical policies of Michael D. Higgins, the former minister for arts, culture and the Gaeltacht, have built up Ireland's potential as a location and base for filming in what appears to be at Scotland's expense. In particular, the filming of much of *Braveheart* in Ireland precisely because of the tax incentives and the burgeoning skills infrastructure stirred Irish-Scottish rivalries. The strong strategic line taken by the Irish Government following Higgins's lead ensured that external investment would provide the commercial and creative development of an indigenous film industry and this approach was much admired and envied, particularly in Scotland. The success of the project, according to Higgins, lay in the integration of 'indigenous energy and the commercial space that tax incentive creates'. The relocation of *Braveheart* provoked huge debate in the Scottish and Irish press, not only in terms of political and economic rivalry, but also about the extent to which the state could and should intervene in the representation of the nation. There was strong interest in the contrast between the influence of the government and that of popular culture and the media, which continually generate, revise and reassert cultural identity in the public arena. At the same time as articulating a mutual jealousy, the debate opened up the possibility for a more open, participative relationship between the cultural and political identities of both communities.

The establishment of a Scottish Parliament in Edinburgh in 1999 was greeted in Scotland as a new opportunity for both Scottish culture and democracy. The Parliament allows Scotland to represent herself internationally, as a multi-faceted modern nation. It is not only a forum for competing political voices, but provides an international medium through which to display the many dimensions of Scottish experience, activity and preoccupations. In

August 1999, the Scottish Executive published 'Celebrating Scotland: A National Cultural Strategy', which prompted many Scottish commentators to consider in practice an idea that they had been debating for more than 20 years, since before the failed devolution referendum in 1979. The cultural strategy was of particular importance because it was the first time that the new Labour government had clearly stated its desire to expand and support film-making in Scotland. According to Duncan Petrie:

> the devolution of political power from Westminster to Edinburgh carried major implications given the increasingly vital role played by public agencies in stimulating and supporting film-making in Scotland. The new Scottish Executive has already given clear indications of its interest in the field ... instigating a new cultural strategy review under the new junior minister for culture, Rhona Brankin. (*Screening Scotland*, 2000)

Sadly, since then, the culture portfolio has been passed around the commutative Scottish Cabinet; Rhona Brankin was shuffled, following Sam Galbraith's resignation, Allan Wilson became a deputy without a boss and a persistent habit of referring to himself as the 'minister for sport' before he departed for pastures greener when he was replaced by Mike Watson, whose interest in the arts element of his remit has been overshadowed by the controversy stirred up by his member's bill to ban hunting with dogs. It seems that the identity of Scotland in political terms is destined to be caught between a discourse of sport and a discourse of culture.

However, all is not lost, as is demonstrated by recent reports to the Education, Culture and Sport Committee of the Parliament on the Scottish film industry, the proposed national theatre and the traditional arts. The film industry report was prepared by Mike Russell, the SNP spokesperson on all things cultural, an independent television producer and strong supporter of Gaelic. Russell's report outlines several key concerns about the industry, particularly in relation to training, fiscal incentives for indigenous and incoming production and the creation of a film-friendly environment. Russell concludes that the central issue is

> the desire to increase the volume of film production in Scotland, both from indigenous producers and from incoming productions with the aim of increasing its economic, social and cultural impact.

In the committee debate on the report, the Conservative MSP Brian Monteith spoke about the possibility of establishing a Scottish film studio at Pacific Quay and questioned whether such a project would 'produce the cultural and financial returns that we would want'. In a more recent debate on the progress of the national cultural strategy, Mike Russell called on the Scottish Executive to deliver on its promise to create a properly funded national theatre and criticised the Executive's strategy for 'failing to gain the support and enthusiasm of the Scottish community'. In the same debate, Brian Monteith suggested that the strategy had 'failed to evoke any substantial response from the people of Scotland who are the ultimate and only source of Scottish culture'. Mike Russell and Brian Monteith rarely see eye-to-eye on any subject (particularly anything relating to state funding or intervention), and their agreement on this issue raises the question of exactly what impacts or returns they were looking for and more broadly, what Scotland hopes to gain from the establishment of an active national film industry and a dedicated national theatre. In Mike Russell's case, it is fairly clear: his political aim is independence and the purpose of a state-supported, strong indigenous industry is to demonstrate Scotland's ability to compete against Britain in the cultural arena. Indeed, in one brief committee debate, Mike Russell managed to relate the desire for a film industry with that for independence three times. Furthermore, the SNP was keen to use images from Mel Gibson's *Braveheart* during the 1997 general election campaign and again in 1999 in the run up to the Scottish Parliament elections. The SNP frequently refers to the *Braveheart* effect, by which it means an increased interest in Scotland and an accompanying increase in sympathy for Scottish nationalism and the independence agenda. I note in passing, that I have never heard an SNP member refer to the *Trainspotting* effect in similar terms. Cultural critics, however, are perhaps more interested in such a possibility. For example, Duncan Petrie talks about *Trainspotting* as forging 'a new sophisticated urban aesthetic' (*Screening Scotland*), which has paved the way for a flurry of energetic, self-consciously British productions.

One key point in Russell's report on the film industry was the impact of the tax concession in Ireland and both the desirability of following the Irish model and the dangers inherent in ignoring it, which he referred to as the Braveheart example. Mike Russell linked such issues to the ability of the Scottish Parliament to raise taxes and the flexibility that would be the result of greater independence from Westminster. In contrast, Brian Monteith described the 'fiscal difficulties that Scotland faces in comparison to the situation in Ireland' as a British problem that required a 'British solution', clearly framing the issue within a unionist agenda. Furthermore, in the debate on the progress of the cultural strategy, Monteith talked about recent drama that 'played to a wider audience' and his amendment stated the Conservatives' confidence that

> Scots culture will continue to flourish without the intervention of the state as it has since 1707.

What that discussion shows is that there are several tensions inherent in what appears to be a shared desire to relocate a national film industry and to support Scottish theatre. First, the cultural value of such an enterprise is confused by the extent to which it depends on economic and social factors, such as training and backing. Secondly, the political identity of such a project is also up for debate, since it can be seen to be used to fit both nationalist and unionist agendas. The commercial nature of the film industry, in contrast to say, that of the novel or theatre, makes the extent to which representation and related activity can be controlled extremely unclear. In other words, what do we mean by what Mike Russell described as the 'economic, social and cultural impacts' of a national industry?

The potential embodied in a flourishing and creative indigenous film industry presents a dilemma to the political bodies that might choose to encourage or emphasise it. Whereas political nationalism seeks to affirm a claim to nationhood underpinned by a coherent history, it must also assert a modern identity that lies outside history, to act as a given that can go beyond the historical moment. Furthermore, the contemporary importance of the nation must be attractive to the national public and provide an economic basis that is sustainable and successful. The welcome expansion of the Irish and Scottish economies in the early 1990s brought with it a boom in the marketing of both countries, and what the market wanted was a return to the romantic, sweeping landscape of *The Quiet Man* (1952) and *Brigadoon* (1954). The traumatic search for a modern identity is a familiar postcolonial problem, but one that is complicated in a cinematic context by the commercial attraction of a ready-made brand. Although the resurgence in Irish film production in the late 1980s began with films that embraced an Ireland that was rooted in the pastoral and the past, such as Jim Sheridan's *My Left Foot*

(1989), and *The Field* (1990), this was followed by attempts to mediate urban, rural and emigrant identity in films such as *Into the West* (1992) and *The Crying Game* (1992). As Martin McLoone has commented:

> contemporary cinema suggests that Irish culture is still obsessed with coming to terms with its rural past, but has still not found an accommodation imaginatively with its urban present. (*Irish Film: The Emergence of Contemporary Cinema*, 2000)

Nevertheless, filmmakers love Scotland and Ireland for their rural landscape, the space that it allows them to project their particular fantasies and, imaginatively, its ability to allow them to visualise the past. However progressive, innovative and dynamic the governments might wish their film industries to be, money, habit and genre all dictate a certain approach. In many respects, film, apparently a progressive and evolving medium, lags behind other cultural forms' rejection of received and rehearsed ideas of national identities. Whereas the Scottish theatre of the 1970s, and 1980s sought to interrogate mythical and historical identity narratives, through plays such as John McGrath and 7:84's *The Cheviot, the Stag and the Black, Black Oil* (1973) to Liz Lochhead's *Mary Queen of Scots Got Her Head Chopped Off* (1987), filmic representations of Scotland have tended to dwell on a lost past and a static present. The reaction of Scottish theatre to the loss of national agency that was confirmed by the failed devolution referendum of 1979 was a critical engagement with collective responsibility and voice. Rather than idolising a Scottish past in which a pure and elevated national identity was shared by all Scots in an uncomplicated fashion, Scottish theatre of the past 20 years has tended to value people's solidarity in the past and their common frustrations in the present. However, as Randall Stevenson, Bill Findlay and others have commented, in many ways, Scottish theatre has suffered for its fragmented and local focus. Although the smaller touring companies such as Borderline, Wildcat and Communicado have had significant success in developing community-based theatre that engages multiple Scottish identities in a broader contemporary cultural context, they have consistently struggled to secure funding, with the majority of the SAC budget going to the national companies—Scottish Opera, Scottish Ballet and the orchestras. In contrast, the Scottish film industry has struggled to get off the ground, various proposals for a purpose-built national film studio have come and gone and the promotion of Scotland as location, rather than nation has seen it host a series of films that replay the familiar elegy for a simple nation corrupted by contemporary culture. Even those few films that could be said to take a critical approach to history, such as *Ill Fares The Land* (1982), have lacked the necessary awareness to overcome the yearning of the 'backward look'. From Hollywood vehicles, such as *Loch Ness* (1995), to UK drama such as *Mrs Brown* (1997) to home grown productions such as *The Bruce* (1996), recent Scottish films frequently play to the idea that the cultural value of Scotland is its past, which bears all the hallmarks of the noble savage. Thus, the production notes of Michael Caton-Jones's film, *Rob Roy* (1995) can boast:

> The Scottish Highlands are virtually unchanged … The making of Rob Roy was a daily adventure of scaling the Highlands, outwitting the weather and recreating a lost and venerable culture.

The releases of *Shallow Grave* (1995) and *Trainspotting* (1996) were broadly welcomed as an antidote to the repeated identification of Scotland with the Highlands and the films have been hailed as providing 'a new emphasis on the city as the heart of contemporary Scottish experience' (*Screening Scotland*, p. 217). Ironically, one of *Trainspotting's* most quoted moments is the only scene shot not in the city, but at Corrour Station, by Loch Ossian:

> It's nae good blamin it oan the English fir colonising us. Ah don't hate the English. They're just wankers. We are colonised by wankers. We can't even pick a decent, vibrant, healthy culture to be colonised by. No. We're ruled by effete arseholes. What does that make us? The lowest of the fuckin low, the scum of the earth. The most wretched, servile, miserable, pathetic trash that was ever shat intae creation. Ah don't hate the English. They just git oan wi the shite thuv goat. Ah hate the Scots.

Renton's expression of self-loathing brings together the masculinist discourse of colonialism (the shame is that Scotland's conquerers are 'effete', thus further undermining the masculinity of Scots) as well as the ambivalence about apportioning blame. Imperialism has consistently presented itself as inherently 'progressive', a civilizing force brought to bear upon backward and incompetent natives. Renton's rant is double-edged: while it rejects the representation of the coloniser as the generous provider of a civilized culture, it retains the image of the colonised as weak and worthless: 'fuckin failures in a country ay failures', as he says.

Why is this passage so popular with academics, film critics, journalists and other trainspotters? In a rather confused review, Harlan Kennedy praises the scene for its subtlety and avoidance of 'signposting':

> The *non-sequitur* isolation of this scene makes sure we understand that while Anglo-Scottish tensions might underlie *Trainspotting*'s story, they lie so far under that like a seismic fault they aren't felt until they produce the occasional, seemingly irrational cataclysm.

Andrew O'Hagan sees Renton's speech as a bold step beyond verbal innovation towards the 'virtually unsayable':

> There aren't many Scottish writers—previous to this generation—who could write such a thing, no films have given voice to this before.

Finally, in an American preview of the film, Anthony Lane wonders how it will play 'stateside', given that the much quoted scene is 'a joke ... a rebuke to the whole tradition of Scottish pastoral, to the hills purple with heather', an assault on the tourist brochure images so beloved by the American public.

For Kennedy and Lane, the strength of this moment lies in its positioning—the single, brief scene in the countryside. Yet this is an invention of Boyle's film; in the novel, Renton's iconoclastic words are to be found in 'The Glass' section, set in a pub on Rose Street, which is about as central as you can get in Edinburgh. What is more, this is no great declamatory speech, but an interior monologue, an anxious and silent deliberation on Renton's relationship with his psychopathic 'pal', Begbie. Commenting on this transposition, Angus Calder observes that:

> the reason [for the relocation] seems to be that the film's audiences south of Scotland will associate the country with Beautiful Highland Scenery. Removed from the complex pattern of interactions in Edinburgh ... Americans and Germans will be challenged to set their romantic conceptions of Scotland against the frustrating reality of modern urban life.

So, for Calder this scene is designed for the benefit of an outside audience (presumably Scots themselves have no need to be challenged by 'the frustrating reality of modern urban life' since they are already living it), with Scotland functioning as an exotic 'other': an object of desire—the beautiful Highland scenery; distaste—the speech itself; and finally similarity—modern urban life. All four critics seem to take Renton's speech at face value, in a way that they wouldn't consider interpreting the scene that takes place in 'the dirtiest toilet in Scotland', for example, or Renton's self-justifications for the resumption of his heroin habit. What all of these critics appear unable to say is that this scene is a rupture in terms of both the film and the book because it claims a direct relationship between individual consciousness and the political status of the nation; something which is overwhelmingly denied by the introspective and self-obsessed junkie narrative. The reaction to this would suggest that any attempt to articulate the social consequences of the ambiguous colonial status of Scotland in cultural production will be subject to a similar form of self-censorship—to be condemned, either for being heavy-handedly prosaic or conversely for a lack of moral standpoint.

The release of *Braveheart* in particular sparked a furious debate between Scottish and Irish intellectuals about the comparative history of the two countries, their relationships to England, and the merits of their respective film industries. Irish critics condemned both the history and aesthetics of the film. Fintan O'Toole, for example, described *Braveheart* as 'historical hogwash', further challenging its integrity by drawing attention to the large amount of filming which took place in Ireland due to tax inducements and the availability of large numbers of extras taken from the ranks of the Irish army. Likewise, Keith Hopper compares the polarised popular and critical reception of *Michael Collins* to 'Mel Gibson's 'Scottish' epic'—placing 'Scottish' in scare quotes to further undermine any claim to national significance. Having first set up the comparison, Hopper then seeks to undo it by claiming Gibson's film as a 'cinematic commodity' in contrast to the artistic and 'political integrity' of Jordan's work. He demands that critics:

> make a commonsense distinction between an international costume drama, which backgrounds history as decorative object; and a national historical drama which foregrounds history as ontological subject.

The desire to separate cultural products along the all too familiar lines of low/high, popular/intellectual is accompanied by an equally familiar appeal

129

to 'commonsense'. Even the terms which Hopper uses to distinguish the two films reflect his prejudices in this area. *Braveheart* is concerned with trivial appearances ('history as decorative object'), whilst *Michael Collins* gets to grips with complex, intellectual issues ('history as ontological subject'). The comments of both Hopper and O'Toole seem to privilege Ireland as a more genuine model of national or nationalist resistance. Furthermore, Hopper's distinction would suggest that a mass audience is incapable of understanding the issues raised by historical drama, implying that *Michael Collins* was less successful commercially because it demanded a more critical and discerning audience. Finally, the projected intelligence of the audience is used to further justify the distinction between the two films on the grounds that Michael Collins is 'art', 'a national event', where *Braveheart* is a Hollywood vehicle. This argument draws attention to an analytical discourse that rejects mobilising forms of identity or even figures of nationhood which are used and developed by working class audiences.

Colin McArthur's position on *Braveheart* would seem to confirm O'Toole's opinion. Roundly condemning the film for historical inaccuracy, moral simplicity and cultural insincerity, McArthur's review tracks specific faults to the discourses of tartanry and 'dark-Ageism':

darkness; religiosity and/or mysticism; grinding poverty and filth; physical deformity; and above all, unspeakable cruelty. These are the dominant tropes of *Braveheart*, although its simple-mindedness also owes something to Errol Flynn's star vehicle, *The Adventures of Robin Hood*.

Like Hopper, McArthur wishes to diminish the cultural significance of *Braveheart* by relegating it to the category of costume drama, where plot and message are secondary to action and style.

What these criticisms fail to take on board is the extent to which both *Michael Collins* and *Braveheart* are created and received in the context of both film genre and national mythology. In a response to McArthur's review in *Sight and Sound*, Sheldon Hall attacks 'his insensitivity to the conventions of genre' and draws attention to the 'narrative tradition' which informs both the style and content of the film:

Linking Mel Gibson's excellent film to the 'regressive discourses' of Tartanry and Dark-Ageism, he neglected to relate it to the equally pertinent—and less odious—discourses of historical romances and mythic epic ... no attempt was made to situate Braveheart within a narrative tradition which also encompasses *El Cid, Spartacus, Ivanhoe, Jesse James and William Tell.*

Despite the value judgments of Hopper and McArthur, the debate identifies both *Braveheart* and *Michael Collins* as 'national events' in the context of a global cultural market.

Could it really be that the financial, economic and social impacts that Scottish politicians were hoping for are, in essence, a form of renewed national democracy? The possibilities inherent in an indigenous film industry require a public engagement in cultural creation that has almost been lost to the political arena. Furthermore, the support for a national cinema provides a practical tool with which to resist what Michael Higgins called 'the colonisation of the imagination', which is brought about by the dominance of the Hollywood studios. Nevertheless, the impact of devolution on the Scottish film industry has so far been negligible. Even the excellent reception of several films such as Lynne Ramsay's *Ratcatcher* (1999) and Peter Mullan's *Orphans* (1999) have failed to stimulate the continued, national funding structure necessary if the industry is to become strong enough to interrogate, engage with and give voice to the identities of Scotland. The political will to support such an industry is dissipated in the compromise of devolution. It is too early to say that the long-hoped-for cultural revolution that would flow from devolution and self-determination has failed to materialise, but the impasse in the development of the national film industry is surely a bad sign. Perhaps it is the theatre where, so far, devolution has had the most significant influence. If so, perhaps Liz Lochhead's *Miseryguts* (2002), a Scots interpretation of Molière's *Le Misanthrope* that mocks Scotland's small array of politicians, celebrities, media luvvies and even playwrights, is in an indication of the tenor of Scottish theatre's reaction to the new Scottish Parliament. Lochhead's misanthrope, Alex Frew, is committed to telling the truth:

'I'm the only person that's not too polite
To tell new devolved Scotland it's a bag of shite.'

NOTES ON CONTRIBUTORS

Ross Alloway is co-editing a collection of nineteenth-century Scottish reviews.

Anthony Carty is Professor of International Law at the University of Derby, having previously lectured in law at Glasgow and Berlin.

Robert Fraser teaches and researches at the Open University.

Christopher Harvie, Professor of British Studies at the University of Tübingen, is the author of *No Gods and Precious Few Heroes*.

Ellen-Raïssa Jackson researches in postcolonial theory and Scottish and Irish literature.

William K. Malcolm is director of the Grassic Gibbon Centre at Arbuthnott.

Gavin Miller is a faculty assistant at the University of Glasgow. He is co-editor of the forthcoming volume *Scotland in Theory*, and is writing a book about R.D.Laing.

Donald Ross is unemployed. He has published fiction in several magazines under a different name, and is working on two novels.

Trevor Royle is a writer and journalist, and an associate editor at *Sunday Herald*.

Ronald Turnbull is co-author with Craig Beveridge of *The Eclipse of Scottish Culture* and *Scotland after Enlightenment*.

Subscribe to *Edinburgh Review*

SUBSCRIBING TO EDINBURGH REVIEW
- Guarantees delivery of the best new writing in Scotland, direct to your door.
- Brings you the best new critical thought in Britain.
- Keeps you informed about the latest work from the small press world.
- Ensures you receive all three issues a year.
- Is still cheaper than buying the magazine in a bookshop.
- Costs only £17 a year for individuals, £34 for institutions.

BACK ISSUES are also available at a discount rate, please contact our office for more information or to place an order.

SUBSCRIPTION FORM

Name:
Address:

Postcode:

I wish to subscribe to the Edinburgh Review, beginning from issue 111/___.
  * I enclose a cheque made for £17 (individual) / £34 (institutional) made payable to 'Edinburgh Review'
  * I wish to pay by Credit / Debit Card, details below:
  [* = delete as applicable]
    Type of Card: VISA / Mastercard / Switch [Delete as appropriate]
    Card Number:
    Card Valid from: _ / _ / _ To: _ / _ / _ Issue No: _ [Switch Only]
Signature:_____ Date: _ / _ / _

Please complete and return form to Edinburgh Review, 22a Buccleuch Place, Edinburgh, EH8 9LN